FROM RELIEF TO EMPOWERMENT

How Your Church Can Cultivate Sustainable Mission

Laceye and Gaston Warner

From Relief to Empowerment: How Your Church Can Cultivate Sustainable Mission

The General Board of Higher Education and Ministry leads and serves The United Methodist Church in the recruitment, preparation, nurture, education, and support of Christian leaders—lay and clergy—for the work of making disciples of Jesus Christ for the transformation of the world. The General Board of Higher Education and Ministry of The United Methodist Church serves as an advocate for the intellectual life of the church. The Board's mission embodies the Wesleyan tradition of commitment to the education of laypersons and ordained persons by providing access to higher education for all persons.

Wesley's Foundery Books is named for the abandoned foundery that early followers of John Wesley transformed into a church, which became the cradle of London's Methodist movement.

HIGHER EDUCATION & MINISTRY
General Board of Higher Education and Ministry
THE UNITED METHODIST CHURCH

CONTENTS

INTRODUCTION

Missional practices flourish in God's reign when they are charac-
terized by hope and mutuality—a difficult but essential balance to
sustain. This book draws upon Scripture, the Wesleyan tradition, and
a Christian nonprofit organization called ZOE (wearezoe.org), which
embodies such a missional practice, to describe faithful and flourishing missional practices for local churches and nonprofit organizations
with mission as their focus. In addition this book acknowledges that
some practices are less than effective—and less than faithful. At times
relief ministries, when offered beyond crisis situations, unintentionally
subvert mutual and hopeful relationships among those with power
differentials—and fullness of life in the reign of God. We hope this
book will serve as a resource for pastors and laity to reflect on faithful
missional practices to discern together and lead others to collaborate
in missions of hope, thereby participating in God's empowerment so
all can thrive in God's reign.

THE SITUATION: RELIEF AND EMPOWERMENT

Over the last approximately one hundred years, an alarming number
of mainline Protestant churches in the United States have disintegrated.
Indeed, the Church as it was known is, for many, over. Admittedly, in local congregations familiar scenes of traditional worship, Sunday school,
and even Christmas pageants, Easter cantatas, and potlucks persist . . .

1

in pockets. However, this question haunts: Are these *really* authentic, generative spaces of the reign of God that share the gospel with a broken, battered, and bleeding world? In so many cases, those planning and participating in these programs have been lulled into a forgetful slumber, disoriented or disconnected from the Church's deep identity and purpose as ordained by God.

Sadly, the Church often relinquishes the core of its identity and purpose to the least common denominator of ministry, avoiding conflict, controversy, and even constraints by focusing tightly on the relief of individuals. Congregations often experience *self-fulfillment* when providing a cup of water to the thirsty, company to the ill and imprisoned, and even mosquito nets to faraway neighbors. While these practices are consistent with the gospel, they do not portray the fullness of the triune God's plan of salvation as described in Scripture. And more pointedly, such practices, when administered *to* rather than *with* individuals and communities not in crisis or enmeshed in complicated socioeconomic ecologies, can actually be destructive.

Christian churches in the United States have at times disempowered their members, neighbors, and communities by defaulting to merely relieving needs, which is a Christian ministry grounded in Scripture, but is not the whole of the message of salvation lived out in communities. According to Robert Lupton, author of *Toxic Charity: How Churches and Charities Hurt Those They Help (and How to Reverse It)*, congregations and nonprofit betterment organizations can "miss the big picture because we view aid through the narrow lens of the needs of our organization or church—focusing on what will benefit our team the most—and neglecting the best interests of those we would serve."[1]

A stark example of misconceptions of the impact of aid and unintended consequences is the story of a mosquito net maker in Africa, told by Dambisa Moyo, author of *Dead Aid: Why Aid Is Not Working*

---

1   Robert D. Lupton, *Toxic Charity: How Churches and Charities Hurt Those They Help (and How to Reverse It)* (New York: HarperOne, 2011), 15.

and How There Is a Better Way for Africa. Mosquito nets are valuable, yet they offer only relatively temporary prevention of the widespread disease of malaria. This mosquito maker manufactures approximately five hundred nets a week. He employs ten people, who (as in many African countries) each support around fifteen relatives. However diligently they work there is always a demand for nets to protect loved ones from malaria-carrying mosquitoes. Unexpectedly, a celebrity or group of celebrities collects and sends a hundred thousand mosquito nets to this same region, at a cost of $1 million. The nets arrive and are distributed, and congratulatory press ensues. However, with the market flooded with free, foreign nets, the African mosquito net maker—and the ten employees—are all immediately out of business. There is no longer work and even modest revenue to support the approximately 150 dependents. Additionally, in no longer than five years, the majority of the nets, whether imported or not, will be torn or damaged, lacking their original effectiveness in preventing malaria infection.[2] The region, though they'd struggled before the importing of the gifted mosquito nets, is left in a much worse and less sustainable set of circumstances after the generous onetime benevolence. This scenario, whether the gift was mosquito nets or other forms of aid (rice, shoes, clothing, corn, etc.), is remarkably familiar to those living in struggling areas, particularly on the continent of Africa.

Christian nonprofit organizations, as well as congregations and their ministries, can move beyond practices of relief in situations that are not experiencing an urgent crisis of emergency by engaging in missions informed by a biblical, theological, and practical rationale for Christian empowerment and relationships of mutuality. This is not to argue for the cessation of all charitable relief and outreach. Victims and even perpetrators of war, violence, oppression, and natural disaster still need the Church's and the world's full attention to provide benevolent assistance. However, Christians and their congregations are

---

2   Dambisa Moyo, *Dead Aid: Why Aid Is Not Working and How There Is a Better Way for Africa* (New York: Farrar, Straus and Giroux, 2009), 44–45.

called by their baptisms to participate in God's reign by reflecting the triune God's love and empowerment, which includes, but moves beyond, relief. This is, after all, how God reaches out to humanity, meeting each person where he or she is. God does not finish with believers at the moment of conversion and justification, but continues to empower them by inviting each into discipleship and sanctification, then calling those to invite others into discipleship. Christians are not simply recipients of God's charity, but God's hands and feet working in the world, because God chooses to invite humanity into partnership in God's unfolding reign.

MISSION IN THE IMAGE OF GOD'S MISSION

To engage in mission is a powerful and wonderful gift. Although sometimes relegated to small committees composed of the willing, when a church fully embraces the power of mission, it tends to inspire, build, and deepen not only the congregation but the entire community. Participating in mission goes beyond accomplishing a checklist of things Christians vaguely feel God wants them to do. To participate in mission is to participate in the *missio Dei*; literally, the mission of God. In the work of mission God allows us to be partners with God in the work of building God's reign on earth, as it is in heaven. We may only achieve glimpses of God's reign in our world, but there is no more powerful privilege and responsibility than to partner in God's own work.

We sometimes define participation in the mission of God too narrowly when speaking about mission in our churches. When bathed in the light of God's mission, what we mean by mission must go beyond simply "we who have much, giving to those who have little." Mission instead becomes living into the image of God. We reach out to others because God first reached out to us. Let us examine how central is this theme of living with others.

Throughout Scripture how we live with one another is placed firmly alongside how we live with God. When the Lord called Abram it was to bless him to be a blessing (Genesis 12:2). "Blessed to be a blessing" is now a rallying cry in churches around the world. Half of the ten commandments outline how we are to live with God, and the other half speak to how we live with one another. Deuteronomy records God's plea to his people to keep God's commands; and in these we see clearly the call of God's people to assist one another, especially those most vulnerable, after the example of God. In a beautiful distillation of the law found in Deuteronomy 10, from which Wesley drew his circumcision-of-the-heart allusion, God mingles the command to love God with the injunctive to serve one another (see verses 16–20). Why must you care for the stranger? Because God cared for you when you were a stranger in Egypt. Why must you care for the orphans and widows? Because they are under the special protection of God, and God will execute justice for them. God has delivered you in every way, and now you are to live in love and justice with one another.

This Old Testament theme is then carried through the New Testament, and Jesus expanded it beyond Israel to include all humanity and all creation. Resisting any pull to simply spiritualize our relationship with God, Jesus repeatedly connected how we live with one another into the center of our spiritual life. How we live with one another is at the very center of what we call mission. Jesus deftly melded the spiritual with the physical in our care for others. When Peter asked Jesus how many times he should forgive another member of the church who had sinned against him, Jesus answered with a story about a king who forgave a great debt for a subject, only to overturn this decision when he found that the subject then refused to forgive a smaller debt to another (Matthew 18:21–35). Not only is how we live with one another important, but it is critical to our following God.

In Luke 10 Jesus praised the lawyer who attempted to test him when the lawyer correctly summarized that the core of God's law is to love God with all your heart, soul, and strength, and to love your neighbor as yourself. When the lawyer sought further clarity about precisely who his neighbor was, to determine where this responsibility to others ended, Jesus responded with the story of a hated foreigner, a Samaritan, acting as a neighbor to a wounded and robbed traveler (verses 25–37). This story explodes the boundaries that define who is

5

one's neighbor. It also informs the contemporary argument about why a church community should assist those in other countries, even when there are plenty of people in need in the communities immediately adjacent to the Church.

Paul further illumined the blessing of mission in Acts 20:35 by quoting Jesus' words, "It is more blessed to give than to receive." In the opening of Romans 15, Paul explained the importance of building up one's neighbor after the example of Christ. In Ephesians 4, Paul's chosen argument to thieves to cease their stealing is so they may "labor and work honestly with their own hands, so as to have something to share with the needy" (verse 28). It is clear in Paul's letters that we are to build one another up, especially those in need, after the example Christ Jesus set for us, and that such work is a blessing to those engaging in it.

To make the argument from Scriptures that love of God and love of neighbor are both central to the Christian life is no great accomplishment. Most people would affirm the truth of such a statement out of hand. However, to follow God's example in engaging in mission also calls us to move beyond simple charity, to something far deeper and more powerful. So often what we call Christian mission takes the form of relief charity. While there is certainly a time and place for such work in addressing emergency situations, such work is not sufficient as Christians' only response to building up their neighbors. When God reaches out to us, our Lord first meets us where we are when we have no ability to turn toward God. However, God then empowers us to move beyond converts to disciples. Certainly God, in Christ, has done for us what we could never have done for ourselves. But God also calls us to become disciples and coworkers in the reign of God. For Christians to engage in mission after the example of the triune God, Christian mission must reach out to assist those who are unable to do anything for themselves but not leave them in that situation. Christian mission must also empower those who are in need so they may begin to meet their own needs, and even in turn to help others who are struggling. In so doing the reign of God begins to grow as leaven in the loaf (see Galatians 5:9).

The building up of one's neighbor is a mutual endeavor. We assist one another, each knowing we may need assistance from others even as we offer such assistance. There is not a "giving" class and a "receiving" class. Rather, we are moving between giving and receiving in many different ways. Scripture does not seem concerned with discerning whether this assistance is physical, spiritual, or psychological in nature but rather paints with a broad brush, assuming each area impinges upon all areas. Scripture addresses the entire person—body, mind, and spirit—to the extent that any modern attempt to separate these into distinct categories is a false separation.

One way to underscore God's mission to us in terms of relief and empowerment is to look at Wesley's categories for how God's grace is poured out to Christians. All grace is initiated by God, but God reaches out to us according to our needs. Prevenient grace is given to us by God before we can even turn to God. Even before we recognize faith in God and our need for God, God is reaching out to us. When we realize our need and turn to God, we experience justifying grace, where we understand and accept Jesus' death as an atonement for our sin. We are freed from the penalty of our sin and justified by the blood of Christ in the eyes of God. However, at that point grace is not finished with us yet. God calls us to move beyond being converts to become disciples. Sanctifying grace works in our lives through the power of the Spirit, leading us toward God's perfect holiness. This grace is a journey that requires our active participation. The power is from God, but God allows and requires us to be partners in our own redemption. We do this by participating in the means of grace, both works of piety and works of charity toward one another.

To engage in mission in the image of God is to treat one another the way God treats us—to follow the example of Christ. Of course, the analogy is not perfect because God is God and we are not, but we do strive to live into the image of God in our interpersonal relationships with one another. If our mission to one another emulates God's mission to us, then ministries of relief must play a part but are not complete in themselves. God reaches out to us before we can do anything for ourselves, but God then calls us to be disciples and then to be partners in the building of the reign of God through reaching out to others. Our mission to others as well may certainly include relief ministries, where

7

the person receives without participating in the process. However, there must come a point where the recipient begins to help himself or herself and, finally, moves to a point where that individual is able to in turn assist others.

After an earthquake, flood, hurricane, tornado, war, famine, pandemic, or other disaster befalling our sin-shattered world, people's lives may have been thrown into disarray overnight. Victims surviving in these emergency conditions need food, water, shelter, health care, and safety. Empowerment ministries in such a situation would be both inappropriate and ineffectual. You cannot empower someone who died because he or she lacked the basic necessities for survival. In such situations relief supplies are needed, and needed quickly, and without a great number of questions and barriers to distributing such supplies.

However, if the survivors of these natural and/or human-inflicted crises continue to receive the same kind of aid three, five, or even ten years down the road, then that relief has failed them. In that amount of time they have moved from being prisoners of a crisis to being prisoners of the aid. What was given to strengthen them in such cases has served only to make them servants; begging replaces dignity, and despair replaces hope. One of the great difficulties we face is that the vast majority of Western aid comes in the form of relief and not empowerment. Since emergency situations are by definition less frequent, one would expect most aid to be in the form of empowerment efforts and relief held for emergency purposes. However, it is understandable why this may not be the case. Relief aid is tangible; it is easy, quantifiable, and we who give the aid feel like heroes. There is the immediate gratification from the perception of having fixed a problem. Relief is important; in a specific context it is the best and perhaps only rational response. But to continue relief where empowerment is needed is to succumb to the siren call of heroism and delusion, over the hard work of addressing the root causes of human suffering. It is easier to build a house than to build a person.

Relief is something we can control. To offer empowerment is to relinquish control of the situation to the recipient instead of the giver. That is hard. Gaston often reflects that where God gets it wrong is in trusting us as participants in our own salvation. In a chain that includes us and God, it is not difficult to spot where the weak links are. We make mistakes, both willfully and out of ignorance. God's trusting us with responding appropriately to God's grace in our lives is certainly where so much goes wrong in the world. For example, to feed orphans is easy. It is easy to do and easy to measure. One can control the entire interaction: how much food is given, its nutritional value, what time of day it is administered, and if one wants to include other helpful practices along with the giving away of food. Given that, Gaston thinks of himself as an imminently sensible person, making the right decisions—maybe even better-informed decisions than recipients have made, left to their own decision-making processes. Again, in emergency situations regarding relief, some of this may be true. In relief situations the needs tend to be clear and basic—food for the hungry, medical care for the sick and dying, heat for the cold, and so on. Speed and action matter in relief work. Economic efficiency and long-term outcomes are less critical. One does not have to think of long-term consequences as much, since a focus on the physical and psychological basics can make the difference between life and death in the short term.

Empowerment work stands in sharp relief to the trauma-room approach to relief. Speed and action can be counterproductive in empowerment work. The short-term or easy fix cannot take precedence over the long-term outcome. Any decision taken away from the person served undermines the core of empowerment rather than bolstering it. Empowerment work may be messy and full of situations, where taking a few steps back may help clear a better path forward. Empowerment involves moving pieces, addressing physical, psychological, social, and spiritual wholeness. In relief work a mistake may have very negative and immediate consequences. In empowerment work a mistake, and the lessons learned from it, may clear a path to a better life.

Just imagine if God were only interested in a relief approach with you and me. What if prevenient and justifying grace were the end of the divine intervention? If God did not rely on our own initiative in growing closer to God and one another, so much of the messiness of our Christian journey would be removed. But it is in the call to discipleship that we learn what it means to serve God. Relief work with those in our human family who have encountered an emergency is critical, but the process to their self-empowerment is also essential so that they may become all that God intends for them instead of being caught in an endless cycle of need, begging for aid. Subsequently, in imitation of God's call for us, those who are empowered in turn become able to empower others.

We must remember in engaging in Christian mission that at its heart, mission work is merely participating in the *missio Dei*, the mission of God. When doing relief work it is appealing to consider oneself the hero and the one who saves, instead of allowing God to occupy that role. When reflecting on a time when you did something to help someone who could not help himself or herself, likely you remember that as a time that made you feel good, useful, kind, even powerful. But in remembering a time when you had to rely on someone else to do something for you that you could not do for yourself, that memory might include a powerless, dependent, or even guilty feeling. Where Paul quoted Jesus as saying, "It is more blessed to give than to receive" (Acts 20:35), we understand the deep truth in that statement. Wesley also took time explaining that the blessing is the one who is able to give to others out of the abundance God has given us.

When doing the messy work of empowerment, it is often easier to see the miraculous work of the Holy Spirit. To receive charity involves a loss of control for the recipient and a realization or seizing of control by the caregiver. Empowerment flips this dynamic so that the recipient has control, and the caregiver must let go. But the letting go of control can free us to experience the work of the Holy Spirit. This kind of missional thinking moves us toward considering the mutuality of mission work, which we will examine further in the following pages.

Empowerment that opens up the possibility of reciprocal relationships strengthening each other under the power of God's Spirit is beautiful to behold. ZOE is one embodiment of such a mission, which aims to empower orphans and vulnerable children in places of greatest financial poverty around the world by helping these children care for themselves. It is sometimes instructive to examine one embodiment of such a mission.

ZOE was originally an acronym for "Zimbabwe Orphan Endeavor," and when ZOE began it was a relief ministry (Zoe is also the Greek word for "life," which is the meaning now ascribed to the organization's name). Several years into its mission, ZOE staff stumbled across an empowerment model, which was more effective by any measure than their previous relief work. This empowerment model was designed by a group of Rwandan social workers, including Epiphanie Mujawimana, who currently directs ZOE's empowerment program in Rwanda.

Epiphanie grew up a semi-orphan from the age of nine, with a deceased father and a physically disabled mother. She worked hard to put herself through school and assist her family.

After surviving genocide as a Tutsi, by the grace of God, Epiphanie felt led to put her strong Christian faith into practice by deciding to spend the rest of her life helping her country recover. She worked for several well-known Western aid organizations, but she soon became disillusioned because she consistently saw her people accept what aid was given, become dependent on that aid, and then be left worse off than before when the grant ran out or the aid moved to another location.

This is when Epiphanie began developing an empowerment model in which orphans (by far the most vulnerable group) could work together to help pull each other out of poverty. These children were working for people in their village in exchange for food. When Epiphanie asked them why they did not grow their own food, they said they did not have a hoe and had no animal to fertilize the land. Epiphanie developed a simple but effective three-year program that provides knowledge and the very basic inputs these children need to pull themselves permanently out of poverty. Topics covered include: food cultivation; hygiene and AIDS prevention; housing; small business training, with micro-grants in year one and micro-loans in year two; education; and vocational training. All this training is done in working groups of sixty to eighty orphans who become an extended family for one another. Most important, the love of Jesus is shared with these children in noncoercive ways, and they are connected with local churches. Now, the gospel message means a lot to you and me; but to African orphans, who feel themselves unlovable, the message of the gospel is like water on desert soil—the gospel is made for African orphans.

Looking at a big group of orphans standing barefoot, someone once asked Epiphanie, "Wouldn't it be great if we could give shoes to all these children?" Epiphanie replied, "Wouldn't it be better if all these children could buy their own shoes?" That is what ZOE is making possible in the lives of these children.

I (Gaston) returned recently from a ZOE trip to Rwanda, where the orphans showed me God's kingdom. One child we visited, Patrick, taught us about reconciliation. We had a group of twenty-two Americans, and we all showed up outside the little coffee shop that Patrick ran. The neighbors were mumbling loudly about something, so Epiphanie, who was translating for us, moved us inside Patrick's shop so we could talk freely. Patrick then began to tell us his story with obvious pride. He was in his second year of the ZOE empowerment program and doing very well. He told us he had been an orphan since he was a young boy and had lived by sleeping in the woods and on the streets at night and working for food in the daytime. Some villagers would give him difficult work to do and would take advantage of him by having him work all day for just enough food to survive, instead of a fair wage. They knew he would have to do whatever they told him because he was desperate.

Living in this way, Patrick had contracted worms and was sick all the time. He was down to sixty-six pounds when ZOE found him and enrolled him in the program. Patrick told us he used his first micro-grant from ZOE to rent land and plant a rice plantation. He was successful in this and made a profit. With his profit and a ZOE micro-loan in his second year, he had opened a village coffee shop, selling bread and milk, tea and doughnuts, and a sorghum drink. Soon after he opened the area health inspector investigated all the food vendors, and Patrick's was the only shop to pass code, since he understood hygiene from his ZOE training. So, with no competition, he expanded and now has several employees—some of whom were the same villagers who used to abuse him by paying him too little for a full day's labor.

Epiphanie asked him what the neighbors had been mumbling about when we first arrived. He said that they were saying, "This boy used to work for us, but now he never will again because he does not need to." Epiphanie laughed at his answer and told us, "This is why I love this program!"

"Yes, they used to abuse me and exploit me," Patrick continued, "but now some of them work for me as employees, and I pay them a fair wage." He does this, Epiphanie told us, because it is what Jesus tells us to do. Patrick taught us that day what it means to love our enemies and repay good for evil.

The next day we visited another group of orphans, who showed us what true Christian sharing is. This working group had come together to build a house for one boy in their group who lived in a mud hut that was falling down. When we arrived, they took a break to greet us and worship with us. As part of their worship the chairman called on several group members to share with us what they had been doing—they had only been in the ZOE program for six months, but you could already see God's hand at work. When they started the program they had eaten about two to three meals per week; now they had at least one meal a day!

Several girls and a couple of boys shared their business venture with us. Each had achieved some moderate success with one business or another—moderate to us but unimaginable to them. But then the chairman called on Gabriel to tell us his story.

Gabriel was fourteen and the sole provider for two younger siblings. He told his story with his eyes downcast. Gabriel had received his micro-grant and had bought supplies for a roadside kiosk selling various small items. One night when he was sleeping, and his younger brother (age ten) guarded the store, two men forced their way in and stole all the supplies. Tears were running down Gabriel's face, tears were running down our faces, and we wondered why the chairman would subject him to the embarrassment of having to tell our group of his failure. But we did not have to wonder long.

After his story was told the chairman told Gabriel the group had something for him. We then watched as the eldest child from each family in the group brought a bag of beans or corn, vegetables, rice, cassava, potatoes, and all kinds of other food. When the procession ended, and as Gabriel stood dumbfounded, spread out in front of him was a pile of food large enough to last him six months, by which time he would be able to try another business. Most of these orphans were eating only one meal a day themselves and could remember going hungry six months before, and yet they gave out of their need to their brother, for all of them had been where he was. Not only did they give, but they rejoiced in the giving because this was the first time many of them had ever been in a position to help anyone else.

I think we get this whole "care for the needy thing" wrong. When God commands us to care for widows, orphans, and foreigners—those who cannot care for themselves—we hear it as a burden. But caring for one another in mutual relationships is the good stuff of our faith; it is what teaches us of God's love for us and about our own faith. We encourage you to heed the message of Deuteronomy 8 to connect your life to the lives of those who depend upon God.

QUESTIONS FOR REFLECTION

1. "Sadly, the Church often relinquishes the core of its identity and purpose to the least common denominator of ministry, avoiding conflict, controversy, and even constraints by focusing tightly on the relief of individuals. Congregations often experience self-fulfillment when providing a cup of water to the thirsty, company to the ill and imprisoned, and even mosquito nets to faraway neighbors." What is compelling to members of a church in simply providing relief? What is good about this? What can be less effective about such an outreach? How is the Church called to do more through following the example of how God calls and empowers Christians?

2. Brainstorm about how the mosquito net distribution in Dr. Moyo's example from her book, *Dead Aid*, could have been conducted in a way that built up capacity. Would such an approach have been

as compelling to donors? Is slow change inherently less exciting than a quick fix? How can people be engaged in the former over the latter?

3. How does it change the conversation to stop thinking in terms of fulfilling our mission, and focus instead on how we can partner with God to accomplish God's mission?

4. Reflect on the draw in our spiritual lives to see faith as having more to do with "my relationship with God," and less with "my relationship with others." How does the Bible call us to be in relationship with both God and others?

5. Here are two mind-sets concerning one's responsibility with regards to God's blessing: (a) "God blesses me; therefore, I must bless others"; (b) God blesses me, empowering me to be a blessing to others; I must therefore bless others in a way that allows God to also empower them to assist others." What is the "return on investment" for each of these trains of thought?

6. If being in mission with one another is truly mutual, what are some of the things that the poor have to offer those who are financially comfortable?

7. What does it mean to say "we participate in our own redemption"? How does this impact the way we go about mission to others?

8. What does it mean to think of relief ministries and empowerment ministries as different and necessary responses to human suffering?

9. Discuss some situations where relief work is most appropriate. Discuss some situations where empowerment work is most appropriate.

10. Reflect upon and describe your feelings surrounding a time when you were able to do something for someone else. Then reflect on and describe a time when you had to depend on someone else to do something for you that you could not do for yourself. How can such thinking inform our view of mission work?

ZOE'S STORY AND GOD'S MISSION

ZOE'S STORY

It is easier to criticize what a ministry does incorrectly than to describe what actually works. Perhaps the latter is a riskier endeavor? Or are there no perfect models? Whatever the reason, it is important to go beyond pointing out insufficiencies and lift ministries up that produce fruit and build the reign of God. Keep in mind that different situations call for varied responses, and there is no panacea to solve all ills. In an emergency, whether a natural or human-caused disaster, relief is the proper response to immediate need. However, in situations of long-term poverty and struggle, one would hope to address the root causes of suffering so that people are able to free themselves from those bonds in a sustainable way. But in any situation the outcomes of the work should be evaluated—and evaluated openly and honestly. Outcomes are different from activities. We measure activities by what is actually done—the number of meals served, inoculations given, houses built, and so forth. Outcomes are what come out of those activities: the results, the consequences in terms of sustainability.

ZOE Helps is one of a growing number of organizations that measure success not by activities but by sustainable and replicable outcomes.

Full disclosure, ZOE is also the organization for which I (Gaston) work. However, I do not use ZOE Helps as an example because I work for them; rather, I work for them because I can use them as an example. Before working for ZOE, I worked for Duke University Chapel, where one of my primary responsibilities was to come alongside nonprofits. I was able to assist with strategy, synergy, cooperation between groups, and connecting them with resources; and I worked with as many as sixty groups a year. I met some incredible people; but with some notable exceptions, I also became somewhat circumspect of the nonprofit social service sector. Great people, great missions, and generous support; but the results and returns on investments rarely lived up to the organizational goals. Much of this failure was due to measuring activities instead of sustainable results.

A majority of organizations engaged in this work in the United States are run by warmhearted Christian folks wanting to do good. Many mission statements are laudable and powerful but bear little resemblance to the actual outcomes of the programs. The organizations often strive toward their missions; but many mission statements are better placed as vision statements, as lofty goals rather than obtainable expectations. So, when I was asked by a longtime friend to come on ZOE's board of directors in 2007, I was more than a little skeptical of ZOE's claims.

ZOE Helps claimed to be an empowerment program able to move some of the poorest orphans and vulnerable children in the world from extreme poverty to generational self-sufficiency in three years or less. I remember thinking to myself, *Well, that is not very likely.* Admittedly, I was no expert on orphans in the poorest areas of the world. I was, however, vaguely aware that this was one of the most intransigent problems on the planet, with numerous atrocities occurring daily as a normal course of business. What an audacious claim to think such a complex system of poverty and oppression could be adequately addressed with a three-year program. I thought perhaps it was another group of good-hearted but somewhat naïve Christians' attempt to do good for poor children without carefully measuring the outcomes. I was utterly and fantastically wrong.

With somewhat low expectations of ZOE's claims but high regard for my friend, I agreed to come on ZOE's board. Although I believe God is working in our world, I continue to be astounded each time I am confronted with God's power in action. The impact of ZOE's empowerment program was such an experience. I did not know that these kinds of results were possible with relatively small inputs. I was also amazed that this program used all the principles that I held to be ideals in a theoretical way but had never seen in action all together: indigenous leadership, ownership by the participants, short-term interventions with sustainable results, avoidance of doing things for people that they could accomplish for themselves, dignity, evangelical outreach without coercion or religious restrictions to participation, and the list goes on. ZOE blew me away. I served on their board and then as staff, and almost a decade later I continue to be amazed by the tangible, measurable results of the program.

Another reason ZOE Helps is a useful program to hold up as an example is because ZOE embodies in its own history the journey that this book and many others advocate—organizations operating in non-emergency situations focusing on sustainable empowerment rather than short-term relief. ZOE began as a relief organization, found a better model for ministry, and transitioned from relief to empowerment. It is this story of changing to a more effective ministry practice, despite all its uncertainly and struggle, that can be helpful to others considering the same trajectory in their own mission work.

BEGINNINGS

Like many movements of God, ZOE began in an unlikely way. A fifteen-year-old young woman was explaining her call to go to Africa and care for AIDS orphans to her loving, supportive, and deeply skeptical parents. First exposed to international poverty through a previous church mission trip to the Bahamas, she began to feel God calling her to ministry with AIDS orphans in Africa after reading about the effects of this pandemic in Africa. There was a two-month mission opportunity where she would spend seven weeks in Zambia and one week in Ethiopia; it seemed perfect. Over dinner this hopeful missionary broached the topic with her parents. Their response was an imminently sensible, "Absolutely not." But she kept at it.

Her mother was the first to crack, finally understanding that it was not just a mission trip but a calling. Her father, however, took a bit more effort to bring around. Finally, after two months of nightly discussions at the dinner table, her father, too, succumbed to this calling and passion for reaching out to orphans.

Although this young lady was unable to communicate with people at home during the two months she worked with African orphans suffering from the effects of AIDS, upon her return she spoke with anyone who would listen to her. Wearing an African dress, she presented to her church many pictures and stories. God used a teenage girl's passion for these suffering children to galvanize her church family and beyond. A group from her church, led by their pastor, then returned to Africa, and her father was on that trip.

This passion spread to the North Carolina Conference of The United Methodist Church. Her pastor spoke with his district superintendent, who had connections in Zimbabwe. In 2004 ZOE Ministry was launched as a relief effort of the North Carolina Conference, with this young person's pastor as the first executive director. What a difference a fifteen-year-old with a calling can make.

As stated in the introduction, ZOE began as a relief ministry. After all, what could African orphans possibly do for themselves? The ministry launched feeding programs, distributed clothing, organized medical clinics, and funded scholarships for orphans to attend school, among other efforts. The 200 million-plus orphans and vulnerable children living and dying in extreme poverty in the poorest countries around the world has been called by some the greatest humanitarian crisis of our age. The North Carolina Conference of The United Methodist Church was proud to have a Christian response to this crisis. The churches in the Conference supported ZOE in generous ways, and the excitement grew.

People supported this new ministry in such a generous way that an interesting problem arose in late 2006. All of ZOE's programs were fully funded, and there was additional funding available. Not wanting to put money in the bank that was given toward an urgent humanitarian crisis,

ZOE decided to put out a call for ministries that were having measurable results in working with orphans in Africa. A minister in the Conference heard a Rwandan social worker named Epiphanie Mujawimana speak at a conference and was intrigued by what she had to say. Introductions between Epiphanie and ZOE leadership ensued, and ZOE began funding Epiphanie's empowerment work alongside their own relief effort.

Epiphanie's own story is quite powerful. At the age of nine, as mentioned briefly in the introduction, Epiphanie's father died in an accident; her mother was physically disabled. Epiphanie began selling vegetables on the side of the road and doing jobs to make money to help support her family and send herself to school. She not only survived; she thrived, becoming a respected schoolteacher in Rwanda.

Epiphanie narrowly escaped with her life and the lives of her two children and her husband during the 1994 genocide. On the other side of that tragedy in her country, she wanted to dedicate her life to helping her people recover, especially the millions of orphans and vulnerable children left in the wake of genocide. She went to work where the resources were, for some well-known Western aid organizations.

Epiphanie worked several years for each organization, but in time she became disillusioned with the work. "I would watch as generous people would come to my country and give my people things they desperately needed," she explained. "I then watched as my people became so good at receiving that they forgot how to do anything." She had invested her life in the lives of people, giving them relief aid; but then, when the focus shifted or the grant expired, she said, "My people were worse off than when I had begun working with them, because they had now developed dependencies upon this Western aid." So Epiphanie and a group of like-minded Rwandan social workers began addressing the needs of the many orphans in their areas in a very different and non-Western way: a form of radical, community-based empowerment, with limited interventions, that relied heavily on resources already present in the villages and communities.

It was this new empowerment model that ZOE began funding alongside its traditional relief efforts. Some were frankly skeptical of

Epiphanie's claim that she had developed a model that could move some of the poorest children on the planet from a place of extreme poverty to sustainable self-sufficiency in just three years, while living in their own villages and learning in a deeper way that they were not beyond the love of God in Christ. However, after funding Epiphanie's work and comparing the results to those of ZOE's other relief efforts, the verdict was clear. In some cases, ZOE's relief efforts made it easier for children to survive in poverty, but Epiphanie's work was helping to address the root causes of that extreme poverty so that children would never need charity again.

And then the Holy Spirit guided ZOE to do an unusual thing; ZOE decided as an organization to pivot away from relief work and come behind Epiphanie's empowerment program because it was more effective.

It may feel strange to say that it is "unusual" for an organization to find an infinitely superior way of working and then adopt that new way in place of older, more ineffectual methods, but that seems to be the case. Organizations such as churches and nonprofits, which do not have income generation as their primary bottom-line goal, may be particularly susceptible to falling victim to doing things in a certain way simply because there has been emotional and financial investment in engaging in ministry in a certain way, even in the face of few measurable outcomes. The term for this human tendency to not want to change is *cognitive dissonance*. Once a person invests in a certain way of accomplishing a goal, that individual is loath to change the chosen path, because he or she has already invested so much in its success emotionally, spiritually, and financially. In spite of all evidence to the contrary, people will continue on an unproductive path to avoid admitting that path may be fundamentally flawed. Christian mission has repeatedly dashed itself upon the rocks of cognitive dissonance. Businesses, too, have this kind of gravitational pull toward the familiar, but the economic bottom line makes change necessary. For ministry, the bottom line can be more ambiguous; and without clear measures for success, success is rarely found.

The prodding of the Holy Spirit allowed ZOE to see a better way of working toward their missional goal of assisting orphans and vulnerable children. ZOE put aside the comparably ineffective methods for the better way to which they had been exposed through Epiphanie's work. ZOE did not conduct this transition in a brash way. Over a three-year period, ZOE began transitioning out of its relief work while ramping up its empowerment work. As part of this process, it tried to move toward empowerment with its former relief partners; but this proved to be a difficult process, both for partners implementing the relief work and for those supporting that relief work. For both groups it seemed that ZOE was abandoning the children who depended upon this aid, instead of moving to a better way of helping these young people in sustainable ways.

This was the first of many lessons ZOE learned about the extreme difficulty of combining relief with empowerment. Once practices of relief are begun, it is very difficult to move from relief to empowerment, though this is often the progression relief agencies vaguely envision when beginning relief efforts. This is part of why one so seldom sees true empowerment in ministries even though eventual *self-sufficiency* may be a stated goal. Organizational teams think, *We will begin with relief and then move to empowerment with our clients.* Such a transitional process makes much more sense in theory than in practice. In practice an empowerment ministry has to be extremely careful not to allow a relief mentality to seep into its program. In a world where most efforts aimed at helping the financially poor are relief based, this is a countercultural move.

MORE SOUP AND LESS STEW

In addition to the Holy Spirit prodding ZOE to move from relief to empowerment, the Holy Spirit also guided ZOE down another unusual path. When ZOE came alongside Epiphanie's African-based model for empowerment, they did not try to fix, improve, or control it. Rather, they relied on Epiphanie and the staff directly involved with the program to be in charge of how the program operated. ZOE in the United States kept a careful eye on fiscal and quality controls but did not interfere in the program itself. Why is this unusual? Westerners tend to have an unconscious assumption that the goal of international missions is to make people more Western. One offshoot of such an assumption is that Westerners tend to see themselves as better equipped than indigenous leadership to make suggestions as to how a program should work. Because this unconscious assumption is often shared on both sides of the missional equation in complex and subtle ways, these unconscious assumptions can be especially corrosive.

At a recent reconciliation event, a seminary student who identifies himself as black South African put it to his U.S. colleagues this way: "When even one Westerner is in a meeting with Africans, the meeting tends to become a stew. In a stew the dominant flavor takes over the dish, even if it is a not a majority ingredient. In this way the Westerner often becomes the dominant flavor in the meeting." He went on to say, "In a soup there are many flavors, but you can still taste each individual ingredient. What we need is more soup and less stew." Most Westerners working in majority world contexts have witnessed this dynamic and, if they are honest, have participated in it, even if at a subconscious level. This is an understandable tendency. I have sat in meetings where I was a cultural minority, thinking the answer to the problem at hand was so very clear. But it was not in fact "clear," or rather my way would not have been the most effective path to address the problem. There were factors at play of which I was wholly ignorant. It has taken years of having this lesson repeatedly demonstrated to me and slowly learning to listen for reasons beyond my understanding or experience to inform the decisions that are made. That is not to say that Westerners should not engage other than through funding. That is like falling off the other side of the cliff, but to listen in a way in which one neither dominates nor disengages is about both art and discipline. It also results in more effective programs.

ZOE was somehow able to avoid this amorphous trap, perhaps as much through ignorance as through a careful philosophical stand. Epiphanie knew what she was doing and had a model that was already successful. This model had so many nuances far beyond the experience of anyone from the United States associated with ZOE that it was both easier and more effective for Epiphanie to be fully in charge of the program. As ZOE expanded from Epiphanie's work in Rwanda to Kenya, Zimbabwe, Malawi, Liberia, India, and Guatemala, this policy improved and was augmented by participants in the program and staff from the countries of service, and then became codified and part of the DNA of the organization. The U.S. staff come up with brilliant ideas every year for improving the program, and it is possible that one or two of these might actually improve the programs, but the others would almost certainly erode the core concepts that make the empowerment model work.

For example, one year the U.S. board was meeting with Epiphanie. She shared how the program participants treasured Bibles, but not every family had one at the beginning of the program. The U.S. board swung into swift action, agreeing that all the children needed Bibles and thinking through the logistics of having native-language Bibles for each program. The board then promptly approved an expense of more than $20,000 to provide a Bible to every orphan-headed family. At the end of this discussion, they asked Epiphanie what she thought. Very gently Epiphanie said, "My one concern is that now these Bibles are treasured by the orphan families in the program. They save and buy them, and these Bibles are a family treasure. I worry that if these Bibles were simply given to them in the first days of the program, I might come to visit them and find that Bible on the floor or neglected, because it was just given to them." A quick scrapping of the previous vote was undertaken.

The U.S. board understood the principles of empowerment, and thus recognized why ZOE strives to avoid doing things for the children that they have the capacity to do for themselves. However, such words are simply platitudes if not put into practice; and putting them into practice is, evidently, very difficult. It is not immediately clear if it is possible for the U.S. staff, board, and volunteers not to interfere when making what they feel are constructive improvements. The slippery nature of this relationship is why the U.S. program has a strict discipline of not offering suggestions for improvement. When volunteers come back from a trip with wonderful ideas of what can be improved, this policy and the reasons behind it are carefully explained. In staying with this discipline, inevitably ZOE loses some ideas that would be very useful. In any given year there may be twenty ideas given, five of which may be truly helpful to the program, and fifteen of which would have unknown ripple effects that would undermine the entire program. ZOE's difficulty is that it may not be possible to know which are the five wonderful ideas and which are the fifteen potential land mines.

An example I like to use of this occurred during one of my earliest ZOE trips to Kenya. The working group of young people had chosen one of their group who was homeless and taking care of many siblings to receive a house from the group. With a grant from ZOE for building materials, the working group was together building a new home for their member. Since our U.S. team was there, the group allowed us to participate—we slowed them down considerably, but they enjoyed showing us what to do and how to go about doing it. Unusually, we had an accomplished builder in our group. He called Reegan Kaberia, the ZOE Kenya director, over to the side and said, "Reegan, there are architectural plans that could help build this home more efficiently and with better quality."

Reegan replied, "I know, but look at the other houses in this village. This is how houses are built in this area. Now look at this family whom the group is helping to build their home. They have been orphaned, homeless, and ostracized from their community. The goal of this home is to help them reintegrate with their neighbors. If we built a different home, even if it was a better structure, neighbors would point to it and say, 'That is the orphan house,' or 'the ZOE house.' This would defeat a large part of the purpose of this house for this family."

What seems like a clear improvement to those of us from the West may actually run counter to empowerment. The goal of the program is not to build houses but to build children.

Empowerment is full of situations where one must take one step back in order for the young participants to take two steps forward. In most non-life-threatening decisions it is better for the participants to try and fail, and then try again and succeed, than for another person to do it successfully for them the first time. Empowerment has goals that are more far-reaching than the immediate task at hand. It is this characteristic of empowerment that may, more than any other single characteristic, make it so very challenging to achieve truly sustainable empowerment.

MISSIO DEI: GOD'S SENDING

The language of *mission* has its roots in the Latin phrase *missio Dei*, or the mission of God. Mission is best understood in light of Scripture and theological foundations as God's "sending," or *missio Dei*. However, the term *mission* has not always been used among Christians to indicate God's sending Jesus and Jesus sending the Church with the Holy Spirit to share the gospel with all creation. Interestingly, for fifteen centuries the Church used other terms to refer to what we subsequently have come to call "mission"—for example, "propagation of the faith," "preaching of the gospel," "apostolic proclamation," and "expanding the church," among others. The latter use of the term *mission* is historically linked "indissolubly with the colonial era." The term continues to assume an established Church, particularly in Europe, that dispatched delegates to convert overseas peoples, specifically in colonial lands, to facilitate European expansion. Therefore, "mission" meant the activities by which the Western ecclesiastical system was extended into the rest of the world.[1]

The emergence of this concept of mission dates to Pope Alexander VI, who essentially divided the non-European world between the monarchs of Portugal and Spain.[2] Similar to previous pronouncements, this action depended on the medieval view that the pope held supreme authority over the globe, whether populated by confessing Christians or not.[3] The power to *send* ecclesiastical agents to distant colonies was extremely influential, leading to the description and roles of these agents

---

1   David Bosch, *Transforming Mission: Paradigm Shifts in Theology of Mission* (Maryknoll, NY: Orbis Books, 1991), 228.

2   Ibid., 227. Bosch was referring to the papal bull *Inter caetera.*

3   Ibid. Bosch explained that this is the origin of the right of patronage (*patronato real* in Spanish and *padroado* in Portuguese), in which rulers had dominion over their lands, including colonies, politically as well as ecclesiastically.

becoming known as the "mission" (a term first used in this sense by Ignatius of Loyola), and the agents themselves as "missionaries."[4]

Developments in world Christianity—namely, its explosive growth in majority world regions—reveal complexities that layer mission history. The fundamental shift of the worldwide geography of Christianity is a critical historical development for the practice of evangelism.[5] Christianity is no longer centered in Europe and the Americas—it is thoroughly worldwide. In 1900, 83 percent of the world's Christians lived in Europe and North America. In 2050, 72 percent of Christians will live in Africa, Asia, and Latin America, and a sizable share of the remainder will have roots in one or more of those continents.[6]

There is unequivocal evidence of some missionaries' capitulation, if not participation, in the oppressive systemic structures of European colonialism. However, in the 1990s, according to Boston University School of Theology's Dana L. Robert, "The icy grip of the 'colonial paradigm' over mission history began to thaw, warmed by an awakening of the realisation that Christianity had become a primarily nonwestern religion."[7]

By the year 2000, more than two-thirds of Christians internationally resided in Asia, Africa, or Latin America, representing one of the

---

4   Ibid., 227–28.

5   Philip Jenkins, *The Next Christendom: The Coming of Global Christianity*, 3rd ed. (Oxford: Oxford University Press, 2001), xi. Professor of missions and world Christianity Lamin Sanneh has also written helpfully in this area, providing a historical as well as a cultural perspective. See Lamin Sanneh, *Disciples of All Nations: Pillars of World Christianity* (Oxford: Oxford University Press, 2008).

6   Jenkins, *The Next Christendom*, xi. "In 1900, the overwhelming majority of Christians were non-Latino whites; in 2050, non-Latino whites will constitute only a small subset of Christians. If we imagine a typical Christian back in 1900, we might think of a German or an American; in 2050, we should rather turn to a Ugandan, a Brazilian, or a Filipino."

7   Dana L. Robert, ed., *Converting Colonialism: Visions and Realities in Mission History, 1706–1914*, Studies in the History of Christian Missions (Grand Rapids, MI: Eerdmans, 2008), 2. According to Professor Robert, "Because of missionaries' strongly held and articulated beliefs in the universal relevance of the Christian gospel, it has been tempting to judge them by their ideas, based on whether the researcher agrees with 'missionary ideals' or disagrees with 'missionary ideologies.' What tends to be overlooked in the history of missions is how the real experiences of missionaries in specific locations, and the concrete needs and interests of early converts, both challenged and shaped the missionary visions themselves" (1).

most dramatic demographic shifts in Christian history.[8] To understand Christianity in non-Western regions, one must explore the ambiguous relationship between Western missions and European imperialism. Although missionary work often preceded European imperialism, inevitably these dynamics pushed missions into an oppressive political space, which some missionaries exploited for their own benefit.[9] On the other hand, missionaries also contributed more constructively through the establishment of missionary schools and hospitals and the training of indigenous teachers as well as doctors and nurses. Robert wrote, "The irony of world Christianity from the Second World War through the 1970s was that even as scholars were writing books implicating Christianity in European imperialism, the number of believers began growing rapidly throughout Asia, Africa, and Latin America."[10] Ultimately, Christianity is more than a politicized Western movement.[11]

MISSIO ECCLESIAE: FROM SENDING TO SENT

Mission, as the phrase *missio Dei* indicates, is rooted in God's actions, in which the church is invited to participate for the sake of the world. As Karl Barth claimed in the opening of his essay on the calling of the Christian community, neither mission nor the church is a starting point in theology. What is at stake is God's witness.[12] The ambiguous relationship between church and mission emerges in Roman Catholic documents such as *Lumen Gentium* and *Evangelii Nuntiandi* (1975) as a result of the Second Vatican Council.[13] Protestants also discussed

---

8 Ibid., 2. See also Dana L. Robert, "Shifting Southward: Global Christianity Since 1945," *International Bulletin of Missionary Research* (April 2000): 50–58.

9 Ibid., 50.

10 Robert, "Shifting Southward: Global Christianity Since 1945," 53.

11 Ibid.: "Indigenous Bible women, evangelists, catechists, and prophets were the most effective interpreters of the faith to their own people." Unfortunately, for a time scholarship in mission history ignored the way ordinary people received the gospel and translated it into cultural modes that met indigenous needs.

12 L. A. Hoedemaker, "The People of God and the Ends of the Earth," *Missiology: An Ecumenical Introduction* (Grand Rapids, MI: Eerdmans, 1995), 160–61. Hoedemaker referred to Karl Barth, *Church Dogmatics*, vol. 4, part 3, 2nd half (Edinburgh: Bloomsbury T&T Clark, 1962), 681ff.

13 Ibid., 161.

similar themes through the world missionary and ecumenical conferences during the middle and later twentieth century, beginning with Willingen in 1952.[14]

In 1952 at Willingen, Germany, the International Missionary Council repositioned a *self-understanding* of church from a sending agency for missionaries to a sent people participating in God's mission.[15] This episode is a turning point in the missionary and ecumenical conversations of the twentieth century, in part because the IMC would eventually merge with the World Council of Churches in 1961. This shift in ecclesial self-identity among international networks of churches was unpacked in subsequent gatherings, including the WCC Assembly in Evanston in 1954 and a study to follow from 1961 to 1967.

The related concepts that "God is the one who sends; church and mission do not have their origin in themselves or in each other but in God's 'missionary' relatedness to the world and humankind" are generally acknowledged among ecumenical audiences.[16] The represented phrase *missio Dei*, therefore, serves a helpful role clarifying the church's vocation and identity in the actions and being of the triune God.[17] Intrinsic to the phrase *missio Dei* is the essential dimension of evangelism.

---

14 Ibid. Hoedemaker highlights Willingen (1952), Melbourne (1980) and their evangelical counterparts at Lausanne (1974), and Pattaya (1980).

15 While the phrase *missio Dei* was not used at Willingen, the shift in *self-understanding* by the church and recognition of its relationship to the Trinity is significant. Hoedemaker, "The People of God and the Ends of the Earth," 163. As Hoedemaker observed, the phrase was used in commentary on Willingen. Hoedemaker prioritized a salvation-historical approach, which leads to his claim that the phrase is confusing. However, Barth and Karl Hartenstein in 1928 and 1934 respectively, as well as Helen Barrett Montgomery even earlier, connected the church's vocation and a deeper concept of mission to the doctrine of the Trinity. See G. Schwarz, *Mission, Gemeinde und Okumene in der Theologie Karl Hartensteins* (Stuttgart: Calwer Verlag, 1980), 130; K. Barth, "Die theologie und die Mission in der Gegenwart," *Zwischen den Zeiten* 10 (1932): 204, 189–215, quoted in Hoedemaker, "The People of God and the Ends of the Earth," 163n.

16 Ibid., 162.

17 Hoedemaker somewhat disagreed, claiming, "A generally current concept (mission) is linked retrospectively with a dogmatic term (missio) that belongs to the theology of the trinity and is used primarily in a passive sense to refer to the 'sentness' of the Son and the Spirit. What is gained by this retrospective linkage is not immediately clear."

Evangelism is the heart of God's mission for the church.[18] By baptism each Christian is commissioned to evangelistic ministry—to proclaim the good news and live according to Christ's example—and initiated into the body of Christ that is sent to the world.[19]

When read as a canonical narrative, mission emerges as a central, if not *the* central theme in Scripture. Not only is Scripture about mission, but the task of biblical interpretation in churches is never complete. Guided by the Holy Spirit, reading Scripture, interpreting texts, and participation in God's reign are ongoing.[20] The Church's mission is not a steadily cumulative process in which readers and hearers progress away from the biblical narratives. Christians are always beginning again from the triune God's salvation narrative that perpetually invites all to receive unexpected possibilities while participating in God's unfolding reign.[21]

Missio Dei describes the inter-Trinitarian action of God's sending Jesus Christ to the world, and Jesus Christ with the Holy Spirit sending the church to the world. Because so many congregations lack a sense of identity and purpose, grounding the practice of missional evangelism, beginning with the triune God, in the interpretation of Scripture for the shaping of practices of missional evangelism—sending and being

---

18 Bosch, *Transforming Mission*, 10–11; Scott Jones, *The Evangelistic Love of God and Neighbor: A Theology of Witness and Discipleship* (Nashville: Abingdon, 2003), 100–101. Jones summarized Bosch's comprehensive discourse on the relationship between the terms mission and evangelism in five statements: "First, mission is wider than evangelism and therefore not to be equated with it. Second, evangelism is an essential dimension of mission. Third, evangelism is witnessing to what God has done, is doing, and will do that aims at a response. Fourth, evangelism is always contextual and relates to the preaching and practice of justice. Fifth evangelism is more than verbal proclamation." Jones, 101, drawn from Bosch, 411–20.

19 For example, see the "Renunciation of Sin and Profession of Faith" in Baptismal Covenants I and II in *The United Methodist Hymnal* (Nashville: United Methodist Publishing House, 1989), 35, 40. The United Methodist reference echoes the ecumenical language agreed upon in the Lima Document: *Baptism, Eucharist, and Ministry* (Lima: World Council of Churches, 1982).

20 Michael Barram, "The Bible, Mission, and Social Location: Toward a Missional Hermeneutic," *Interpretation* (January 2007): 42.

21 Richard Bauckham, *Bible and Mission: Christian Witness in a Postmodern World* (Grand Rapids, MI: Baker Academic, 2003), 21.

sent is a helpful starting place. God's mission gives purpose to the people of God, or community within history through whom God works toward the goal of blessing the nations. In the canonical Scriptures this community refers to Israel in the Old Testament and the church as the messianic heirs of Israel in the New Testament. Again, the phrase "people of God" is used to describe a people existing for God's purpose.[22]

QUESTIONS FOR REFLECTION

1. Do you agree with the statement that "it is easier to criticize what a ministry does incorrectly than to describe what actually works"? When is it helpful, and even necessary, to criticize ministries? And when is it unhelpful? What makes criticizing a ministry more challenging than criticizing a business practice or similar endeavor?

2. In our ministries how do we separate traditions that help preserve our faith and commitment to God's reign on earth, as it is in heaven, from traditionalism, which can lock us into ineffectual or even harmful ministry practices that limit the fruit of our ministry?

3. In practice it is extremely difficult for an empowerment ministry to keep relief from seeping into their program. Why might this be the case? How can good intentions by those attempting to assist others be counterproductive to long-term success for the participants?

4. Have you ever been in a discussion where people had different worldviews? What did you learn about your own set of assumptions regarding how things should work in a specific context?

5. What changes between thinking about mission as something we do because God wants us to do it and thinking that when doing this work we are participating in the mission of God? Is this just a difference of semantics or something deeper?

---

22 Christopher J. H. Wright, "Covenant: God's Mission Through God's People," in *The God of Covenant: Biblical, Theological and Contemporary Perspectives*, ed. Jamie A. Grant and Alistair I. Wilson (Leicester: Apollos, 2005), 55.

FROM RELIEF TO GOD'S EMPOWERMENT

BEYOND RELIEF

Nearly 90 percent of adults in the United States are involved personally or financially in the charity industry.[1] What is surprising is that the outcomes of this involvement in the "charity industry" are almost entirely unexamined.[2] Why is it that when people with business and financial backgrounds engage in outreach they fail to apply the basic principles of viability of their fields, and they default instead to traditional models of charity?[3] Numerous examples demonstrate the persistent dilemma that "when relief does not transition to development in a timely way, compassion becomes toxic."[4]

Robert Lupton, the founder of Focused Community Strategies Urban Ministries, is a practitioner as well as an author committed to embodying, and helping others embody, healthy Christian relationships across

---

1   Lupton, *Toxic Charity*, 2.
2   Ibid., 3.
3   Ibid., 17–18.
4   Ibid., 6–7.

socioeconomic boundaries. Lupton bases much of his argument on firsthand experience and practices but also builds upon the work of economist Dambisa Moyo. In her book *Dead Aid*, mentioned in the introduction, Moyo makes a compelling argument for the damage caused by large-scale aid when not given during times of crisis. Moyo describes three types of aid: (1) humanitarian or emergency aid, "which is mobilized and dispensed in response to catastrophes and calamities"; (2) charity-based aid, "which is dispersed by charitable organizations to institutions or people on the ground"; and (3) systemic aid, "that is, aid payments made directly to governments."[5] Moyo quotes recipients of systemic government aid to support her case—one echoed by Rwanda's President Kagame in an interview with *Time* magazine in September 2007: "Now the question comes for our donors and partners: having spent so much money, what difference did it make? In the last 50 years, you've spent US$400 billion in aid to Africa. But what is there to show for it? And the donors should ask: what are we doing wrong, or what are the people we are helping doing wrong? Obviously somebody's not getting something right. Otherwise, you'd have something to show for your money."[6]

Senegal's President Wade also made similar remarks, stating in 2002, "I've never seen a country develop itself through aid or credit. Countries that have developed—in Europe, America, Japan, Asian countries like Taiwan, Korea, and Singapore—have all believed in free markets. There is no mystery there. Africa took the wrong road after independence."[7]

Moyo offers messages to aid recipients and providers. She urges aid recipients to:

> Get off aid.
> Promote entrepreneurship.
> Promote free trade.

---

5   Moyo, *Dead Aid*, 7.

6   Ibid., 148–49.

7   Ibid., 149.

Invest in infrastructure.

Secure reasonable loans, not grants.

Encourage stable homeownership.

Moyo also offers a message to nongovernmental religious organizations:

Don't subsidize poverty.

Reinforce productive work.

Create producers, not beggars.

Invest in self-sufficiency.[8]

A key principle of efficient community development is: "Never do for others what they can do for themselves."[9] This shift is profound and affirms the value and dignity of all those created in the image of God. "Forging ahead to meet a need, we often ignore the basics: mutuality, reciprocity, accountability. In doing so, relationships turn toxic."[10] Lupton claims those who have worked among the poor for any length of time will recognize the following pattern:

Give once and you elicit appreciation.

Give twice and you create anticipation.

Give three times and you create expectation.

Give four times and it becomes entitlement.

Give five times and you establish dependency[11]

It is far easier to improve a betterment program that serves people by providing charity than to build a system of organizations and opportunities that empowers them.[12]

---

8   Ibid., 96–97.

9   Mary Nelson, *Empowerment: A Key Component of Christian Community Development* (Bloomington, IN: iUniverse, 2010), 64. Nelson cites Saul Alinsky, the father of community organizing. Lupton echoes this principle in his description of the "shift from doing for to doing with" in Lupton, *Toxic Charity*, 29.

10   Lupton, *Toxic Charity*, 57.

11   Ibid., 129–30.

12   Nelson, *Empowerment*, 33.

Community development basics describe the following formula: "First stop, relief . . . Second stop, rehabilitation . . . Third stop, development."[13] John McKnight, founder of the widely respected asset-based community development movement, claims that "services rarely empower the poor because (1) they divert money away from poor people to service providers, (2) programs are based on deficiencies rather than capacities, and (3) services displace the ability of people's organizations to solve problems."[14] McKnight and others in community development ask for candid answers to the following questions:

- Does the activity recognize the mutuality of participants as children of God—in the body of Christ?
- Does the activity strengthen the capacity of those in need?
- Will the activity be self-sustaining and even wealth-generating for those in need?
- Do resources generated (especially financial) stay in the community and with those in need?
- What is the timetable for transitioning the ownership of the activity to the local community and those in need?[15]

Asset-based community development focuses on asset mapping, while not dwelling on deficiencies. Asset mapping identifies resources in individuals and the community to align these to frame a constructive strategy for collaboration and mutuality. "This approach unleashes new resources and a whole new sense of abundance, providing a starting place for empowering action."[16]

An asset-based approach helps to:

13   Lupton, *Toxic Charity*, 138.
14   Referenced by Lupton, *Toxic Charity*, 144–45.
15   Adapted from Lupton, *Toxic Charity*, 145.
16   Nelson, *Empowerment*, 40.

- identify and mobilize the assets of individuals and institutions, especially those who are "clients" of social services
- build relationships among community members and institutions, especially those that are mutually supportive
- give community members more roles and power in local institutions, resulting in citizen-led efforts[17]

Building relationships of authentic mutuality between those of unequal socioeconomic power is careful and delicate work.[18] As a response to arguably desperate situations of disempowerment and dependency, a result of toxic charity, Lupton proposes an Oath for Compassionate Service. "These well-tested principles, applied to service work, point individuals and organizations toward practices and partnerships that empower those we wish to assist."[19]

The Oath for Compassionate Service

Never do for the poor what they have (or could have) the capacity to do for themselves.

Limit one-way giving to emergency situations.

Strive to empower the poor through employment, lending, and investing, using grants sparingly to reinforce achievements.

Subordinate self-interests to the needs of those being served.

Listen closely to those you seek to help, especially to what is not being said—unspoken feelings may contain essential clues to effective service.

Above all, do no harm.[20]

---

17   Ibid., 55. Activities that enhance journeys toward empowerment include: asset-mapping, prayer walks, listening conversations, and making connections (56).

18   Lupton, *Toxic Charity*, 37. "But relationships built on reciprocal exchange (what I call holistic compassion) make this possible."

19   Ibid., 8.

20   Ibid., 8–9.

UNDERSTANDING GOD'S EMPOWERMENT

There are a number of working concepts of empowerment—some more helpful than others. From a corporate management perspective, empowerment may be understood as "a motivational process that can influence employee perceptions of power relations, leadership styles and motivation in the work place."[21] This category of empowerment seeks to maximize productivity, capacity, and morale in the workplace. Interestingly, there is research in this area of study acknowledging the lack of attention regarding "the role that empowerment played in [Jesus'] relationships with his disciples."[22] Perhaps a relative extreme to a corporate use of the term is the understanding of empowerment as deeply spiritual, even Pentecostal or charismatic, within and sustaining meaningful Christian lives and mission.[23]

Another set of themes related to empowerment is more disparate, emerging from the widespread usage of such language among, for example, nongovernmental agencies and human rights organizations and includes concepts such as process, strategy, and outcomes. Empowerment is generally considered closely related to the concept of

21 A. J. H. Thorlakson and R. P. Murray, "An Empirical Study of Empowerment in the Work-place," *Group and Organizational Management* 21, no. 1 (1996): 67–83. Quoted in Stacy Hoehl, "Empowered by Jesus: A Research Proposal for an Exploration of Jesus' Empowerment Approach in John 21:1–25," *Journal of Applied Christian Leadership* 2, no. 2 (Summer 2008): 5. In this area of study, further research reflects on "the empowerment process as focusing on three areas of follower development, including confidence and self-efficacy, values and beliefs, and work-related skills." Hoehl goes on to unpack each of these categories.

22 Hoehl, "Empowered by Jesus," 16. According to Hoehl, "Through the exegetical analysis tool of inner textual analysis, Jesus' empowerment approach was analyzed with respect to John 21:1–25. In this section of Scripture, Jesus' actions offer insights into his empowerment strategies set forth in the leadership literature. Jesus' empowerment approach consists of developing his disciples' confidence and self-efficacy, challenging their values and beliefs, and equipping them with the skills needed for their ministries."

23 For a discussion of the former, see David A. Dorman, "The Purpose of Empowerment in the Christian Life," *Pneuma: The Journal of the Society for Pentecostal Studies* 7, no. 2 (Fall 1985): 147–48. For the latter use regarding mission, see Eddie Gibbs, "The Launching of Mission: The Outpouring of the Spirit at Pentecost," *Mission in Acts: Ancient Narratives in Contemporary Context* (Maryknoll, NY: Orbis Books, 2004), 18–28.

power: how to understand, define, and distribute power.[24] Liberation theologies are often called upon to argue for empowerment as a new generative theme.[25] This can be a helpful starting place but presents constraints as well.

The language of empowerment is often used as a substitute for development in the sense of transferring social, political, and economic power for the purpose of justice for individuals in communities.[26] For example, "Empowerment can be understood as the language of the oppressed to claim the rights they have been denied."[27] This could lead one to focus on the scarcity or at least limited availability of power among humans to provide needed resources for survival. In the New Testament Gospels, Jesus Christ clearly confronted powers of injustice and evil. However, the goal was neither an isolated confrontation as an end in itself nor solely an anthropological focus but gestures toward redeeming, restoring, and reconciling relationships with God and neighbor, or even the oppressor, for vital living within an eschatological frame. While social, political, and, economic justice is clearly a goal of a biblical, theological embodiment of Christianity, there is also an aspiration for reconciliation with God and neighbor, providing space not merely for survival but for flourishing in an abundance of God's grace and mutuality within the reign of God.

A helpful frame within which to construct an understanding of God's empowerment is a biblical, theological consideration of Christian community development based in relationships of mutuality. Community development, which aligns with neighborhood empowerment, is that which strengthens a neighborhood's capacity to become self-sustaining.[28] Empowerment ultimately is about the transfer of power. At

---

24 Mery Kolimon, "Empowerment: A New Generative Theme of Christian Mission in a Globalized World," *Exchange* 40 (2011): 37.

25 Ibid., 35–56.

26 Ibid., 38, 50.

27 Ibid., 37.

28 Nelson, *Empowerment*, 31.

its best, empowerment depends on two things: that power can change and expand.[29]

This understanding of empowerment resonates with a Christian conception of God's grace. John 15:15 demonstrates Jesus' calling his disciples into a different kind of relationship: "I do not call you servants any longer, because the servant does not know what the master is doing; but I have called you friends, because I have made known to you everything that I have heard from my Father."[30] The charity approach can communicate the message that the poor require changing their lifestyle, spending patterns, and so forth. Such a message inadvertently communicates that those suffering from poverty are somehow diminished. This is in direct contradiction to the gospel message that God created each in God's image and that God indwells and loves each one of us in an unfathomable way.[31]

Empowerment moves from servanthood to friendship for the purpose of living out the reciprocal nature of mutuality in friendship.[32] "The charity approach also creates a distance between people, making it hard to have a relationship—much less a genuine friendship."[33] Participating in God's empowerment is at a most basic level shifting from doing for to doing with[34] to enjoy the mutuality and abundance of God's grace. According to Lupton, "It is delicate work, I have found, establishing authentic parity between people of unequal power. But relationships built on reciprocal exchange (what I call holistic compassion) make this possible. . . . It is infinitely more difficult to detoxify existing relationships than to build new, healthy, reciprocal relationships between rich and poor."[35]

---

29   Ibid., 61.
30   Ibid., 28.
31   Ibid., 27.
32   Ibid., 31.
33   Ibid., 27.
34   Lupton, *Toxic Charity*, 29.
35   Ibid., 37–38.

PARTICIPATING IN GOD'S EMPOWERMENT?

This section provides some background and potential next steps when participating in God's empowerment in mutual sustainable relationships across socioeconomic abilities. While there are numerous examples of opportunities for individuals, congregations, and organizations to pursue, this section focuses on two: short-term mission immersion experiences and care for orphaned and vulnerable children. Both of these examples benefit from substantial research and data providing assessment of the impact of particular practices of relief and empowerment.

Other opportunities also exist for shifting betterment efforts to empowerment opportunities in expanding and deepening participation in God's reign. It is important to consider that some relief programs, when not responding to an urgent crisis, may benefit from closing to reallocate time and financial resources in more fruitful methods of ministry. Efforts to administer charitable or benevolence giving could be rechanneled into micro-lending opportunities and/or a job bank;[36] a clothes closet could be restructured into a thrift store or a food pantry into a food cooperative.[37] These initial relief and betterment services, when not responding to an urgent crisis, may offer a more helpful impact when shifted to include recipients as participants through long-term strategies that provide employment, experience, and opportunities to participate in God's many dimensions of salvation. Such efforts tend to be even more effective when couched in a supportive Christian community made up largely of those struggling to make a better life.

---

36 For example, see Nobel Peace Prize-winner Muhammad Yunus's *Banker to the Poor: Micro-Lending and the Battle Against World Poverty* (New York: Public Affairs, 1999, 2003); and David Bornstein, *The Price of a Dream: The Story of the Grameen Bank* (Oxford: Oxford University Press, 1997).

37 An excellent resource for launching such endeavors is David Bornstein and Susan Davis, *Social Entrepreneurship: What Everyone Needs to Know* (Oxford: Oxford University Press, 2010).

Short-Term Mission Experiences

Approximately 32 percent of U.S. congregations provide opportunities for international mission trips each year, with 41 percent of American teens reporting participation in a mission trip or religious service project.[38] Clear, substantial data exists to demonstrate the impact of short-term, particularly repeated, mission experiences on the beliefs, practices, and vocational discernment of adolescents and young adults participating in such trips. However, the impact of such experiences into adulthood is a topic needing further attention.

Participation among adolescents in domestic short-term mission trips has "a significant, positive influence on the likelihood of volunteering for either a local or an internationally focused organization as an adult." Interestingly, though, participation of adolescents in short-term domestic mission trips has a significant "dampening effect on charitable giving to secular organizations."[39] While missional travel experiences may incline participants toward a particular trajectory, without additional influence the experiences have no long-term impact. Demographics, childhood socialization, social networks, and milestones seem to matter more.[40]

The practices and goals of short-term mission experiences cover a wide spectrum of diversity, while sharing some common themes. Mission trips require departure from one's local community, usually for less than two weeks and may be undertaken annually by some. Practices and goals of these experiences vary, from including evangelism, to providing services, cultural immersion, education, and/or social justice advocacy. However, the most common practice of short-term mission experiences is execution of a service project.[41]

Despite the focus on service projects or humanitarian aid of some kind, and contrary to broad assumptions, most mission trips do not:

---

38   LiErin Probasco, "Giving Time, Not Money: Long-Term Impacts of Short-Term Mission Trips," *Missiology: An International Review* 41, no. 2 (2013): 203.

39   Ibid., 202.

40   Ibid., 203.

41   Ibid., 204.

empower those being served, engender healthy cross-cultural relationships, improve quality of life for those served, relieve poverty, change
the lives of participants, or increase support for long-term mission work.
Unfortunately, they often do weaken those being served, foster dishon-
est relationships, erode recipients' work ethic, and deepen dependency.[42] Even more sobering, according to Lupton, "If we listen to those on
the receiving end of these service projects, we see a different picture
emerge. Most work done by volunteers could be better done by locals
in less time and with better results."[43] Lupton unpacks his argument: "The
overwhelming majority of our mission trips are to places where the
needs are for development rather than emergency assistance. And development is about enabling indigenous people to help themselves. This
requires a longer-term commitment, not the sort of involvement that
lends itself to short-term mission trips."[44]

This is not to say that mission trips are unimportant or entirely counterproductive. The main point of this section is to clarify the impact and
effectiveness of short-term mission experiences, domestic and international. For the time and expense it seems prudent to understand as ac-
curately as possible, with the assumption that research and data draw
upon specific circumstances, both the intended and unintended consequences of our claims and practices. Short-term mission trips, particularly when reinforced by other dynamics and experiences, are incredibly
impactful upon adolescent and young adult beliefs, vocational discernment, and inclination to volunteer. However, short-term mission trips in
most cases are not effective strategies to relieve systemic poverty.

What about Orphanages?

Throughout the biblical canon, particularly in the Old Testament, the
people of God and participants in God's reign are invited, even urged,
to care for widows, orphans, and strangers. When we consider the

---

42   Lupton, *Toxic Charity*, 15–16.

43   Ibid., 16–17.

44   Ibid., 69.

most vulnerable of humanity, whether in the time of the Old and New Testaments or today, children without parents, secure shelter, food, or health care—much less spiritual nurture, education, and sustainable income—emerge immediately. While there are abandoned and vulnerable children in the midst of the plague of poverty, which impacts every region and culture, the most vulnerable and widespread seemed to be those related to the AIDS pandemic in sub-Saharan Africa.

Each day approximately 6,000 Africans die from AIDS. An additional daily 11,000 are infected—many, if not most, of these are parents of countless children.[45] In one revised estimate from 2000, there are currently 34.7 million children under the age of fifteen in thirty-four countries who have lost their mother, father, or both parents to HIV/AIDS and other causes of death. By 2010 that number was estimated at 44 million. Without AIDS, the total number of children orphaned would have declined by 2010 to fewer than 15 million. In 2010, 20 to 30 percent of all children under fifteen will be orphaned in eleven sub-Saharan African countries, even if all new infections are prevented and some form of treatment is provided to slow the onset of AIDS in those infected with HIV.

AIDS and HIV have reached epidemic proportions in many developing countries. It is serious enough for the United States to consider it a threat to its national security, and in some nations the epidemic has had a large impact on mortality rates and the economy. UNAIDS estimated that for 2008 worldwide there were:

- 33.4 million living with HIV

- 2.7 million new infections of HIV

- 2 million deaths from AIDS

---

45   Lester R. Brown, "HIV Epidemic Restructuring Africa's Population," *World Watch Issue Alert* 31 (October 2000). The remaining statistics in this paragraph are taken from FHI and USAID, *Care for Orphans, Children Affected by HIV/AIDS and Other Vulnerable Children: A Strategic Framework* (Arlington, VA: Family Health International, June 2001), 2. This work was supported by the United States Agency for International Development (USAID).

Approximately 7 out of 10 deaths for 2008 were in sub-Saharan Africa, a region that also has more than two-thirds of adult HIV cases and more than 90 percent of new HIV infections among children.[46]

This tremendous need, particularly when witnessed firsthand, provokes earnest responses and sacrificial gestures of assistance. The most familiar and traditional model for caring for children is the orphanage or children's home, which occurs in most areas of financial poverty, many with histories linked to the colonial and mission eras. However, comprehensive research by organizations seeking accountability for and effectiveness of aid, particularly in sub-Saharan Africa, are generating unequivocal results demonstrating the lack of effectiveness and even unhelpful results of the orphanage model. USAID, the largest aid program with significant resources for researching effectiveness, released findings as early as June 2001 that began a shift from relief to empowerment in the recommended care of abandoned and vulnerable children in sub-Saharan Africa.[47]

Care provided in institutional settings often fails to meet the developmental and long-term needs of children, and orphanages are much more expensive to maintain than providing direct assistance to families and communities to care for orphaned children themselves. The experience of major international child welfare organizations shows that children benefit greatly from the care, personal attention, and social connections that families and communities provide.[48] Particularly in the majority world, where the extended family and community are the primary social networks, the absence of such connections greatly increases long-term vulnerability. Children raised in orphanages often have difficulty reentering society once they reach adulthood. As a result of long-term experience with orphanages, several countries independent of the U.S.-based research led

---

46 Source and further details: *AIDS Epidemic Update 2008, UNAIDS and WHO*, November 2009.

47 USAID, *Project Profiles: Children Affected by HIV/AIDS* (June 2001), 3.

48 FHI and USAID, *Care for Orphans*, 7, 9.

their governments to shift approaches from traditional orphanages to family-based care.

Costs associated with providing basic care to orphans increases exponentially when salaries, building maintenance, and food storage and preparation are required. Cost comparisons conducted in Uganda show the ratio of operating costs for an orphanage to be fourteen times higher than those for community care. A 1992 study by the World Bank found that institutional care at one facility in Tanzania cost $1,000 per year per child, a figure six times more expensive than the average cost of foster care in that country. Other studies have found a ratio of 1:20, or even up to 1:100. In communities under severe economic stress, increasing the number of spaces in orphanages often results in families deciding their children can be better served by orphanages than at home.[49] "Long-term institutionalization of children in orphanages and other facilities is not a desirable solution to the impacts of HIV/AIDS. Resources expended to fund institutional care for a single child can assist scores of children if used effectively to support a community-based initiative."[50]

There is a shift in many countries to eliminate orphanages or greatly restrict them because of their ambivalent impact. It takes a good deal of negative results for countries to do away with traditional systems of care, but orphanages seem to have provided ample negative results over a long period of time.

Major problems include the following:

- Orphanages are extremely expensive and are often outside interventions (funded and frequently overseen by foreigners to the indigenous culture).

---

49 USAID, *Children Affected by HIV/AIDS*, 3.

50 FHI and USAID, *Care for Orphans*, 9. "The institutionalization separates them from families and communities and often delays healthy childhood development. FHI's priority is to strengthen communities to continue to care for their children and facilitate the reintegration of children into families and communities, making sure that health and viable living arrangements can be made."

- Orphanages are often filled by non-orphans through the actions of desperate parents.

- Skills development for sustainable living as an adult are often lacking.

- Foreign churches tire of raising endless money to support orphanages with little tangible results in terms of lives changed.

In majority-world nations, the extended family and community at large traditionally provide care for orphaned children. To reinforce this tradition, an alternative model for institutions has involved transformation of children's homes into community-based resource centers that help families support children in the community. Such centers provide day care for foster parents or parents in need of relief, support groups, counseling, training in parenting skills, and skills training programs for older children.

"Strengthening the capacity of communities to fill the widening gaps in the safety net traditionally provided by the extended family is what FHI sees to be the most efficient, cost-effective, and sustainable way of assisting orphans and other vulnerable children. Families and communities also play a crucial role in the identification of children who are most in need, both those affected by AIDS and other vulnerable children."[51]

Where circumstances prevent a family from providing immediate care, institutionalized care is best used as a temporary measure until more appropriate placement can be arranged.

ANOTHER WAY?

Donata has an overwhelming story. As with so many orphans in Rwanda, both her mother and father passed away from AIDS-related

---

51   Ibid., 7, 9. "Community members know best who these children are and what their needs are, and through a process whereby they identify them and building their capacity to improve their well-being, responsibility and ownership are increased, stigma attached to being an 'AIDS orphan' is decreased, and children who are most in need are attended to" (9). See also Jon Singletary, "Hope for Orphans: A Model of Care for Vulnerable Children," Baylor School of Social Work: Family and Community Ministries, 29–38. Singletary's article includes a helpful bibliography.

illnesses, during which time their mud hut collapsed; so, at age five, Donata was left both orphaned and homeless. But she was also left with a three-year-old sister and a six-month-old baby to care for. It would be difficult for us to imagine our own children surviving in this situation, but somehow Donata did. There are tens of millions of Donatas in our world today living and dying in extreme poverty. Children are raising children. It has been called the greatest humanitarian crisis of our age, and we think that is in no way an overstatement.

After somehow surviving ten years in this situation, first begging for food and shelter, and later begging for work and being paid in food, at fifteen Donata joined ZOE's program. She took to the ZOE training immediately. She then started several businesses and trained as a seamstress. She was a leader in her group, providing for her family and speaking in churches about what God had done in her life. Then she seemed to regress.

Concerned, her group members informed the ZOE program facilitator that Donata seemed to be tired and hungry again. The facilitator spotted the problem immediately: Donata had adopted six additional orphans. When the facilitator asked her why, she said she had not meant to. "They were living on the streets, and I invited them in for a meal but they would not leave—and I remembered what it was like to be where they were. I thought, *How can I speak in churches about the power of God and turn my back on these children?*" Donata explained.

Donata's group, upon hearing this, decided to build a large home for her; and after several months her new family had stabilized. What is more, the children she had adopted were now beginning businesses of their own and enrolling in school.

Christian nonprofit organizations, congregations, and their ministries need to move beyond practices of relief outside an urgent crisis situation by participating in mutual relationships of Christian empowerment.[52] This is not to argue for the cessation of all charitable relief and

---

52 See Moyo, *Dead Aid*; and Lupton, *Toxic Charity.*

outreach. As previously mentioned, victims, and even perpetrators, of war, violence, oppression, and systemic poverty, as well as natural disasters, still need the church's and the world's full attention to provide benevolent relief. Rather, Christians and their congregations are called by baptism to participate in God's reign by reflecting the triune God's love and empowerment to us, which includes, but moves beyond, relief to encourage and support Christians in relationships of mutuality.[53] There are additional issues to which congregations need to attend for faithful participation in God's reign—discipleship, pastoral care, formation, worship, and sacraments. However, alongside these there is a need for practicing healthy reciprocal relationships within and beyond the body of Christ. Empowerment is a response to the triune God's act of redemption in Jesus Christ through the Holy Spirit pulling the doer and receiver closer to God and each other by creating a collaboration that respects each party's contributions and gifts in the midst of God's unconditional grace.

QUESTIONS FOR REFLECTION

1. If so many charitable works are conducted without the benefit of careful measurement of outcomes and return on investment, but much of the support and oversight (boards) of such charity are made up of professional people regularly employing such measures, why is it that these disciplines are not used more often in charitable work? If discussing in a group, argue for and against, or split up the group and have half argue for this situation and the other half argue against; then come together to discuss the issue freely.

2. Senegal's President Wade stated in 2002, "I've never seen a country develop itself through aid or credit." The same sentiment could

---

53 This is not to argue that there are not problems with empowerment language or that there needs to be a balance between antinomianism and Pelagianism. Christian empowerment is also not to be confused with the prosperity gospel.

be applied for a large majority of individuals. Why would this be the case? Where are the proper places for aid and credit? Why would Robert Lupton say a primary precept of empowerment work is, "Never do for others what they could do for themselves"? Read Lupton's "Oath of Compassionate Service"; discuss and consider adopting it as a guideline for yourself and/or your church.

3. What is the highest purpose of a short-term mission trip, once it is accepted that such trips have little empowerment benefit (building a home or school could be done more economically and efficiently by locals; even education is better placed locally in most cases, etc.)? What are the good effects a short-term mission trip can have? How does one avoid seeing a short-term mission trip more as an experience for the missioner than a lasting benefit to the beneficiaries? How does one evaluate the results of a mission trip, beyond a warm feeling?

4. It is difficult to move beyond traditional approaches to mission, even when there is little evidence of effectiveness. Why is this the case? How can one lovingly help people to see better ways of engaging in ministry? Why is this such a painful journey in so many instances?

JOHN WESLEY'S PRACTICES OF EMPOWERMENT

John Wesley is well-known for his leadership of the eighteenth-century Methodist renewal movement within the Church of England. Although not unique, his ability to hold together divergent theological emphases empowered Methodism as a movement. John Wesley insisted on the importance of combining works of piety with works of mercy as means of grace. Wesley went beyond simply teaching and preaching to also organizing an effective structure by which people were held account-able in the pursuit of a sanctified life. A central component of Wesley's expectations of works of mercy, which has been underemphasized, was his response to the socioeconomic context of his time through the practice of wealth sharing. Wesley personally pursued, and required of those adhering to the Methodist movement, a strict expectation that Christians were to engage in economic sharing, to the extent that to fail to share one's overabundance with those in need was to steal from God. Moreover, Wesley did not leave his vision of works of mercy with simply wealth sharing but built structures to facilitate the empowerment of the poor to live sustainable and flourishing lives.

JOHN WESLEY'S CONTEXT

Although poverty has existed in every society in one form or another, the idea that poverty is a social or political problem to be addressed, and fixed if possible, is a recent phenomenon.[1] Scholars attempting to uncover and illuminate Wesley's economic ethic must take his context into account, not as a peripheral part of his theology, but as its backdrop. To look at Wesley's economic ethic through modern lenses is to risk distorting that ethic.[2] All theology is culturally shaped, but Wesley's social ethic was particularly and purposefully praxis driven. This makes setting Wesleyan theology in historical context particularly crucial.

So, what was the cultural context of Wesley's ministry? The eighteenth century was a time of tremendous economic and social transition. With the birth of the Age of Enlightenment, eighteenth-century England emerged as the leader of industrial capitalism. This was a time of turmoil but also of opportunity for the poor. Wesley wrestled with how these changes fit into his economic ethic, or rather how he could encourage himself and others to live into the image of Christ. Some

---

1   Richard P. Heitzenrater, ed., *The Poor and the People Called Methodists* (Nashville: Kingswood Books, 2002), 9.

2   Theodore W. Jennings Jr., *Good News to the Poor: John Wesley's Evangelical Economics* (Nashville: Abingdon Press, 1990), 16, 18, 19–20. Theodore Jennings has been ensnared by this temptation in his book *Good News to the Poor*. Jennings makes several statements for the purpose of co-opting the eighteenth-century Wesley as a proponent of a twentieth-century agenda. Jennings claims exemption from a careful historical study of Wesley and the context of the eighteenth century by claiming that he is a theologian interested only in the modern interpretation of Wesley. The effect of such a stance is not to free Wesley from the chains of historical irrelevance but rather to put modern words and ideas in the mouth of Wesley. Jennings has begun an important conversation that would benefit from careful historical understanding. For helpful approaches and appropriation of historical consideration of Wesley, see Scott J. Jones, *United Methodist Doctrine: The Extreme Center* (Nashville: Abington Press, 2002), 28; Randy L. Maddox, "'Visit the Poor': John Wesley, the Poor, and the Sanctification of Believers," in Heitzenrater, *The Poor and the People Called Methodists*, 59–60; and Jose Miguez Bonino, "'The Poor Will Always Be with You': Can Wesley Help Us Discover How Best to Serve 'Our Poor' Today?" in Heitzenrater, *The Poor and the People Called Methodists*, 184–85, 187. For example, Jose Miguez Bonino, another Methodist scholar writing from a liberation perspective, offers modern extrapolations of what Wesley has to say to our modern context but does so while taking the contextual differences of time and place seriously.

of his contemporaries attempted to clarify the radical social changes taking place. Wesley's writings about the larger economic forces at work with the poor, including *Thoughts on the Scarcity of Provisions* (1773), were roughly contemporary with Adam Smith's publication of his well-known work, *Wealth of Nations* (1776). In this work Smith described the rise of capitalism without using that term.[3] While Wesley and Smith had very different thoughts concerning the ultimate goal of economics, Smith advocated the retention of wealth as the basic means of acquiring even more wealth. However, Wesley encouraged the gaining of capital so it could be shared among the reign of God.[4]

During this time of great transition in both thought (enlightenment) and economics (the birth of industrial capitalism), there was also a great shift in how the poor were viewed and the way they came to see their own future possibilities. At the beginning of the industrial revolution, there was a huge influx of people from the rural areas into the major cities. Cities offered the possibility of jobs in manufacturing. However, the cities also offered multiple forms of drinking, gambling, and other corruptions to which the poor, in an attempt to escape the miseries of daily life, were particularly susceptible.[5] Although there had always been some religious response to the poor in Britain, in the sixteenth century there was a shift from individual almsgiving to a more national, tax-financed program to relieve the poor in response to a period of unsuccessful crops and economic hardship.[6]

Such a concept of relief for the poor included a limited number of specific conditions but was expanded in the seventeenth century in terms of numbers assisted, the kinds of people helped, and the depth of public support for such programs.[7] This gave rise to the establishment

3   Bonino, "'The Poor Will Always Be with You,'" in Heitzenrater, *The Poor and the People Called Methodists*, 188.

4   Maddox, "'Visit the Poor,'" in Heitzenrater, *The Poor and the People Called Methodists*, 62.

5   Thomas A. Langford, *Practical Divinity: Theology in the Wesleyan Tradition* (Nashville: Abingdon Press, 1998), 1:15.

6   Heitzenrater, *The Poor and the People Called Methodists*, 16–17.

7   Ibid., 17.

of the *Elizabethan Poor Laws*. These laws were written as a response to the growing idea among the wealthier classes that poverty was a social problem to be alleviated for the greater good of society. This feeling achieved broad public support by the time Adam Smith clearly articulated it in the 1776 *Wealth of Nations* as a social and, more important, economic problem.[8] Richard Heitzenrater, professor of church history and Wesley studies, described the evolution of the process: "What started in Elizabethan England as an attempt to reform and remodel systems of charity was followed by a Jacobean tendency in the seventeenth century to see the problem in terms of the national economy—poor relief should be purposive and discriminatory. By the eighteenth century, the whole system had become a social program of national welfare."[9]

In the seventeenth century there were some attempts to establish institutions to combat poverty, such as charity hospitals, schools, orphanages, and other organizations aimed at primarily helping those in need. This trend was greatly increased in the eighteenth century.[10]

Although there had been many advances with regard to public and private systems for alleviating poverty in the seventeenth and eighteenth centuries, there remained a powerful and negative social stigma associated with asking for or accepting assistance. Many poor would refuse public assistance, viewing the "dole" as shameful, and people continued to be whipped for the illegal activity of begging as late as 1782. Having said this, the situation of the poor had been highlighted; and the sense of a responsibility, or at least enlightened self-interest, to care for the poor was meeting with a slowly increasing sense of entitlement by the poor themselves. This growing sense of entitlement by the poor and enlightened self-interest by the rich for solving the poverty problem resulted in an interesting division. The poor increasingly viewed the relief provided by the Poor Laws as a right, while the wealthy viewed it as a burden to be undertaken only if it fostered positive results and

---

8   Ibid., 18–19.
9   Ibid., 19.
10   Ibid., 22.

the general economic situation improved.[11] However, the urban poor of Britain were excluded from the established Church in much the same way that they were excluded from established society.

JOHN WESLEY AND THE POOR

John Wesley and the nascent Methodist movement at Oxford gained a reputation for ministering to and visiting with the poor. Whether leading services in local workhouses, jails, or individual homes; working with the elderly, or the youth; fund-raising on behalf of the poor; or offering advice, assistance, and care, the Methodists gained a reputation for helping the poor, and this reputation was not altogether a positive one.[12] John Wesley ministered to people who were unlikely to be in contact with the established Church through his work with the poor and imprisoned at Oxford, and later, beginning in April 1739, through field preaching to thousands of people.[13] Wesley's enthusiastic application of what he viewed as a clear biblical mandate for ministry earned him and the other Methodists derision from fellow students, among others.

Some scholars assume that Wesley actively sought out the poor and established his ministry almost exclusively for their benefit. This is misleading. Wesley was interested in imitating the life of Christ, a life that included ministry with the poor and rich alike. Wesley was extremely reluctant to engage in the socially distasteful practice of field preaching, where many of the urban poor first heard his message, and finally succumbed as a result of the repeated prodding of his colleague George Whitefield. Only after Wesley witnessed the great success of this strange practice of preaching outdoors did he admit that such a base practice could be used by God for good and therefore was acceptable. Wesley was not chasing after the poor but rather imitated the life and practices of Christ. This life attracted great numbers

---

11 Ibid., 23.
12 Ibid., 26–27. It was in this derisive spirit that the nickname *Methodists* was applied to the overly enthusiastic revivalist group.
13 Langford, *Practical Divinity*, 1:15.

of the population that were formerly estranged from the established Church.[14]

The attempt to portray Wesley as actively seeking out the poor is not completely inaccurate, in that Wesley did strive to put into practice the biblical teaching of Jesus through clothing the naked, visiting the sick and imprisoned, feeding the hungry, and other means of grace. These practices were a living out of the dual biblical commands to love God and neighbor. For Wesley, the communal act of loving one's neighbor through meeting his or her physical, social, and spiritual needs was important both to those giving and to those receiving such care. This was true regardless of whether the caregiver or receiver was wealthy or poor. Wesley called the Methodists to live a life that emulated Christ. This life was to be lived inside the bounds of the established Church, to include love of God and love of neighbor, and to incorporate both faith and works. The people who responded to this profoundly simple, yet elusive, synthesis of orthodoxy and orthopraxis were overwhelmingly the disenfranchised working poor—who comprised over half of the general population.

It was unnecessary for Wesley to seek out the economically disenfranchised; they were all around him. He did not demonstrate a preferential option for the poor, but the poor responded to Wesley's message of sacrificial living in a way that the wealthy largely did not. One might say that the poor had a preferential option for Wesley, or more specifically, Wesley's message of imitation of Christ. In Methodist theology the poor were able to find a means by which they could be partners in their own charity. With the social stigma "of being on the dole," a societal perception that the poor were lazy and less moral than others, and a system of belief where the poor were expected not only to receive help from their brothers and sisters, the expectation to offer the "widow's mite" was empowering and life-giving to many of the poor. The patients

---

14   Heitzenrater, *The Poor and the People Called Methodists*, 27. Heitzenrater puts the point in context. "To say, as some do today, that Wesley had a 'preferential option for the poor' is simply to say that he did not categorize more than half of the population as outsiders (as 'them'), as the Church seemed to do."

became the cure, but sacrifice and transformation were required, and the life-giving source was Christ. The poor became partners with God and with one another.

Wesley's definition was fairly consistent throughout his ministry: the poor were those people who did not have enough to meet the basic necessities needed to live, such as food, clothing, and shelter. This definition was not unique to Wesley but was a common benchmark in the eighteenth century.[15] Wesley chose this qualitative measure instead of employing more quantitative economic figures.

The Elizabethan Poor Laws set the measure for poverty as not having adequate shelter. Since basic tenement housing would be approximately £10 per year, and housing was one-third of a person's total yearly expenses, it is reasonable to set £30 per year, or 2s. 6d. per day as a quantitative poverty line.[16] This would equate to roughly £2,800 ($4,480) in modern terms.[17] If such a figure is accepted, then those in poverty would have included more than half the English population in 1760.[18] The Methodists included a slightly higher percentage of people earning under £30 per year, estimated at around 65 to 75 percent, with only 25 percent of Methodists earning above this figure.[19] These statistics highlight that while the poor were drawn to Wesley, he did not have to make special efforts to reach this group. Wesley welcomed the poor and the wealthy alike, and both groups came, although the wealthy had other, more respectable, options, such as the established Church. Notably, the established Church did not have a policy of exclusion concerning the poor, and there were benevolent ministries taking place in the Church. However, in a wider society that looked upon the poor with disdain, they were denied access in subtler ways. Without access to proper education, dress, manners, and

---

15   Ibid.
16   Ibid., 18.
17   Ibid., 20.
18   Ibid., 27.
19   Ibid.

speech, many felt out of place in a Sunday morning service in their local parish.

JOHN WESLEY'S MINISTRY WITH RICH AND POOR

Wesley was not interested in providing a systematized outline of his own economic ethic; however, by examining oft-repeated themes, the careful reader can find four cornerstones of Wesley's message concerning wealth and possessions: (1) the source of all things is God, so all things belong to God; (2) earthly wealth has been placed in human hands to be stewarded on God's behalf; (3) God expects that we use what we are given to provide for our own necessities and then the necessities of others; and (4) to spend our God-given resources on luxuries while others are in need of necessities is to misuse what God has given us.[20]

This economic ethic was not theoretically new, but Wesley was concerned that it be practiced and perfected among those who strove to live in imitation of Christ. In Wesley's sermon "On Use of Money," he outlined the proper actions of a Christian toward wealth in his famous, and often misused quote, "Gain all you can, without hurting either yourself or your neighbor . . . Save all you can, by cutting off every expense which serves only to indulge foolish desire . . . Give all you can, or in other words give all you have to God."[21] This is not, as is sometimes claimed, an endorsement of laissez-faire capitalism as outlined by Adam Smith.[22] On the first two points—make all you can and save all you can—Wesley is in line with Smith's advice that people acquire capital. Even on the third point that once wealth has been acquired it must be used to best advantage, John Wesley and Adam Smith are in agreement. Wesley, however, turned this budding economic theory on its head with his last instruction to give all one can. For Wesley, money

---

20 Maddox, "'Visit the Poor,'" 62.

21 John Wesley, "The Use of Money," in *The Works of John Wesley*, vol. 2, Sermons II: 34–70, ed. Albert C. Outler (Nashville: Abingdon Press, 1985), 278–79.

22 Maddox, "'Visit the Poor,'" 62.

is used to best advantage by being employed to meet the basic needs of one's neighbor and not simply as a tool to accumulate more wealth. In a world where the rich get richer, Wesley railed against excess accumulation as theft from God.

John Wesley implemented a strict definition of wealth accumulation. As we have seen, wealth is a gift from God, supplied to humanity to meet basic needs (food, shelter, clothing) and then to be given to others to assist in meeting their basic needs. Wesley saw this ordering not as a reasonable system of secular communalism but rather as the requirement of God, lived out in the example of Christ. In his sermon "The Good Steward," Wesley made this connection explicit:

> But first supplying thy own reasonable wants [necessities], together with those of thy family; then restoring the remainder to me [God], through the poor, whom I had appointed to receive it; looking upon thyself as only one of that number of poor whose wants were to be supplied out of that part of my substance which I had placed in thy hands for this purpose; leaving the right of being supplied first, and the blessedness of giving rather than receiving?[23]

It is a significant point that one restores the gift of money to God through the poor. Once again Wesley had made clear the spiritual dimension of providing for physical necessities and the physical dimension of the spiritual life and growth. People who claim Wesley as a proponent of the capitalist or Marxist model must first understand the lens through which Wesley saw the use of money. Money is a gift from God that is used for God's purposes. These purposes are outlined in Scripture and modeled in the life of Christ. Wesley was interested in larger political structures only insofar as they assisted or hindered Christians living into the reign of God in this life and the next.

It is because the reign of God was at stake in these arguments that Wesley implemented such a strict definition of what money was to be used for. To spend money on oneself and one's family, beyond meeting

---

23   John Wesley, "The Good Steward," in Outler, *The Works of John Wesley*, 2:295.

the necessities of life, was to steal from God.[24] Wesley summarized this in his sermon "Upon the Lord's Sermon on the Mount, X": "Let our superfluities give way to our neighbour's conveniences (and who then will have any superfluities left?); our conveniences, to our neighbor's necessities; our necessities to his extremities."[25] John Wesley, like many of his contemporaries, relativized the concept of poverty. Rather than speaking of poverty as a certain quantity or level of income, as we do today, Wesley offered a sliding scale according to needs and desires that included superfluities, conveniences, necessities, and extremities.[26] Wesley's view of what constituted necessities was more than what wealthy contemporaries of his day thought the poor deserved (by including enough food to sustain health, clothes that qualified as decent and clean, and adequate housing) but less than what we think of today.[27] It does seem that by the 1760s Wesley had softened his stance and indicated that it was permissible to accumulate a bit beyond the bare necessities of life as long as this was not the primary goal being pursued.[28]

Wesley implemented this teaching to the best of his ability. In addition to speaking consistently about the necessity of both giving to and interacting with the poor, Wesley required that Methodists practice this discipline. Added to Wesley's impressive personal record of giving, outlined in detail throughout his diaries, Wesley demanded that his followers give generously and often, even when they themselves stood on the brink of poverty. John Wesley was so bold and so constant in his requests for money to be used on behalf of the poor that his younger brother, Charles, complained, "How many collections think you has my brother made between Thursday evening and Sunday? No fewer than

24 See Wesley's sermon "On the Danger of Increasing Riches," at the Wesley Center Online, http://wesley.nnu.edu/john-wesley/the-sermons-of-john-wesley-1872-edition/sermon-126-on-the-danger-of-increasing-riches/.

25 John Wesley, Sermon 30, "Upon Our Lord's Sermon on the Mount, X," S26, *Works*, 1:662; quoted in Heitzenrater, *The Poor and the People Called Methodists*, 28.

26 Ibid., 36.

27 Ibid., 29.

28 Ibid., 30. Another interesting note is that when Wesley married, he greatly relaxed his stance on accumulation.

seven. Five this one day from the same poor exhausted people. He has no mercy on them, on the GIVING poor I mean; as if he was in haste to reduce them to the number of the RECEIVING poor."[29]

Wesley was more interested in spiritual revival than in large numbers and in obedience to the example of Christ rather than popularity. This stringent policy eroded slightly over time and was greatly relaxed after Wesley's death, a situation he predicted as he neared the end of his life.[30] As Methodism became increasingly respectable and middle-class, the movement put less emphasis on living a disciplined life of prayer, service, and economic sharing. As the movement became less strict, the numbers of Methodists swelled, but the sense of being separated from the world as citizens of God's reign was also greatly diluted.

Giving to those in need was not just a magnanimous gesture on behalf of the rich to succor the poor; it was a deep spiritual discipline that carried spiritual benefit to both the giver and the receiver. Wealthy and poor alike were expected to participate in this discipline. In this way John Wesley universalized the response to poverty; all were expected to offer assistance, even the poor themselves, including the widow with her mites.[31]

LOVE OF GOD AND NEIGHBOR

Love of God and neighbor are held at the very center of John Wesley's ministry and serve to balance and guide all other parts. For Wesley, it is possible for a person to pursue both works of mercy and works of piety and yet not be a Christian, if the impetus for such actions and practices is not love—both of God and of neighbor. In his *An Earnest Appeal to Men of Reason and Religion*, Wesley made this point abundantly clear in writing to those who live a moral life by living rightly and practicing the means of grace but without love. "You may go thus far, and yet

---

29 John Wesley, *A Plain Account of the People Called Methodists*, XIII.2, *Works*, 9:277, quoted from Gareth Lloyd, "Eighteenth-Century Methodism and the London Poor," in Heitzenrater, *The Poor and the People Called Methodists*, 126.

30 Bonino, "'The Poor Will Always Be with You,'" in Heitzenrater, *The Poor and the People Called Methodists*, 184.

31 Heitzenrater, *The Poor and the People Called Methodists*, 36.

have no religion at all—no such religion as avails before God . . . You have not the faith that worketh by love."[32] Wesley's conception of true religion was grounded completely in love, and from this wellspring the outer trappings of religion receive meaning. According to Heitzenrater, "Methodism moves beyond a lifeless, formal religion to one worthy of God, and that is love—love of God and love of neighbor, seated in the heart and showing its fruits in virtue and happiness."[33]

Wesley carefully articulated his acceptance of the doctrine of *sola fide*.[34] It is not that Wesley was uncertain that faith was necessary for salvation; rather, that such faith must work through love to be grounded in God. And if grounded in God, this faith manifests itself in good works both of piety in relation to God and of mercy to one's neighbor. Wesley proclaimed this necessity consistently throughout his ministry. In one of his last sermons, "The Wedding Garment," from March 1790, he stated, "The imagination that faith supersedes holiness is the marrow of antinomianism."[35] This statement strongly asserts that simple mental acquiescence to the truth of the gospel does not ensure that there has been an inner transformation of the individual.

Randy L. Maddox, in *Responsible Grace*, points out that Wesley navigated a course between the Roman Catholic emphasis on good works and the Protestant insistence on salvation by faith alone. Maddox quotes Wesley's sermon, "The Law Established by Faith": "We are doubtless 'justified by faith'. This is the corner-stone of the whole Christian building. . . . But [the works of the law] are an immediate fruit of that faith whereby we are justified. So that if good works do not follow our faith, even all inward and outward holiness, it is plain our faith is nothing worth; we are yet in our sins."[36]

32 Quoted in Richard P. Heitzenrater, *Wesley and the People Called Methodists* (Nashville: Abingdon Press, 1995), 131.

33 Heitzenrater, *Wesley and the People Called Methodists*, 130.

34 *Sola fide* is Latin for "faith alone."

35 Heitzenrater, *Wesley and the People Called Methodists*, 307.

36 Randy L. Maddox, *Responsible Grace: John Wesley's Practical Theology* (Nashville: Kingswood Books, 1994), 175.

Wesley's favorite passage on this point was Galatians 5:6, "For in Christ Jesus neither circumcision nor uncircumcision counts for anything; the only thing that counts is faith working through love." Wesley was convinced both that faith is something that God does for us out of God's love and that this faith empowers us, through the Holy Spirit, to act on behalf of others.[37] Therefore, all good works, whether works of mercy or works of piety, flow from this central place—love of God and love of neighbor. It is impossible to separate the two since each requires the other. One cannot love God without loving his or her neighbor, and to love the neighbor is also to show love to God.

A tendency to truncate the richness of Wesley's theology of faith and works can be seen in contemporary Methodism. People unwittingly separate Wesley from his insistence upon personal piety by claiming he was an unqualified proponent of liberation theology and social gospel over and against personal piety. Wesley's quote that "there is no holiness but social holiness," taken from his "Sermon on the Mount," is often called upon to prove Wesley's supposed priority of works of mercy over piety. However, by putting the quote in its wider context, it becomes clear that Wesley's point was the importance of the Christian's pursuit of the holy life.[38] One cannot be a Christian in isolation from others; rather, the love of God requires the love of others. This is certainly not in opposition to either liberation theology or social gospel, but it requires that personal piety also be present to inform and practice works of mercy.

ORIENTED TOWARD GOD: HOLY TEMPERS

Wesley consistently emphasized the need for good works but also recognized that a merely mechanical engagement in good works without the proper inner disposition of the heart did not lead to a sanctified life. If the disciple did have the proper inner disposition of the heart,

---

37 Ibid. For more on empowerment by the Holy Spirit, see *A Plain Account of Christian Perfection* (1766) at the Wesley Center Online, http://wesley.nnu.edu/john-wesley /a-plain-account-of-christian-perfection/.

38 Maddox, "'Visit the Poor,'" 63–64.

affections, or holy tempers, then the believer would be guided toward the inner transformation that led to a sanctified life and external actions that embody such a life.[39] For Wesley, the tempers, unlike affections, are much more solid and represent a "fixed posture of the soul" or a proven orientation toward holy behavior.[40] Wesley described this fixed inner stance in his *Explanatory Notes upon the New Testament Regarding 1 Thessalonians 2:17*:

"In this verse we have a remarkable instance, not so much of the transient affections of holy grief, desire, or joy, as of that abiding tenderness, that loving temper, which is so apparent in all St. Paul's writings toward those he styles his children in the faith. This is the more carefully to be observed, because the passions occasionally exercising themselves, and flowing like a torrent, in the apostle, are observable to every reader; whereas it requires a nicer attention to discern those calm standing tempers, that fixed posture of his soul, from whence the others only flow out, and which peculiarly distinguish his character."[41]

According to Wesley, such holy actions did not come naturally or by a desire of our will, but they must be formed and initiated by holy tempers.[42] It is appropriate that love of God and neighbor proceed from holy tempers in Wesley's theological framework because Wesley considered love to be the foundational temper from which all other tempers flowed.[43] It is God's will that love becomes the ruling temper of the believer's soul, and only when this inner transformation takes place can the Christian's actions be propelled by, in Wesley's words, a "habitual disposition of the heart."[44]

---

39 Maddox, *Responsible Grace*, 178.

40 Kenneth J. Collins, *John Wesley: A Theological Journey* (Nashville: Abingdon Press, 2003), 147.

41 Ibid., 146–47, quoted from John Wesley, *Explanatory Notes upon the New Testament* (London: William Bowyer, 1755; repr., Grand Rapids: Baker, 1987), 1 Thess. 2:17.

42 Maddox, *Responsible Grace*, 178.

43 Ibid.

44 Ibid., quoting from Wesley's sermon "The Circumcision of the Heart," in *Works*, 1:402–3.

WORKS OF MERCY

Works of mercy include acts of compassion to and from one's neighbor. It is significant that Wesley at times emphasized works of mercy above works of piety, such as prayer, worship, and fasting.[45] This emphasis was purposeful as a corrective to the exclusion of works of mercy as means of grace in traditional Anglican theology. Works of mercy were encouraged but did not hold the emphasis in traditional Anglican theology that Wesley placed upon them. For Wesley, the means of grace were so vital to the overall framework of how to live into the life of Christ because they mediated the love and grace of God in a special way. Practicing such works was not a nice addition to one's real purpose of being pious; for Wesley, these works were central to living out the grace-filled life.

The physical need for works of mercy for the one receiving them is often obvious; but for Wesley, these acts of mercy were also a channel of God's grace for the person offering compassion.[46] Through encountering one's neighbor the disciple also encountered God. This is the power of Wesley's theological framework that ultimately drew it beyond a simple matter of distinguishing orthodoxy and orthopraxis as two distinct actions; for Wesley, they are intimately and inseparably intertwined.[47] In Wesley's letter to a Miss March, he answered her objection that practicing works of mercy curtailed her available time to practice works of piety. He did this by highlighting both the example of Christ and the biblical mandate to engage in works of mercy that Wesley followed in his own life.

> Yet I find time to visit the sick and the poor; and I must do it,
> if I believe the Bible, if I believe these are the marks whereby

---

45 Joerg Rieger, "Between God and the Poor: Rethinking the Means of Grace in the Wesleyan Tradition," in Heitzenrater, *The Poor and the People Called Methodists*, 86. This is based on Wesley's Sermon 92, "On Zeal," II.5, *Works*, 3:313.

46 Rieger, "Between God and the Poor," in Heitzenrater, *The Poor and the People Called Methodists*, 87.

47 Ibid.

> the Shepherd of Israel will know and judge His sheep at the great day …

> … I am concerned for you; I am sorry you should be content with lower degrees of usefulness and holiness than you are called to.[48]

As stated earlier, for Wesley to practice works of piety without also practicing works of mercy was disingenuous. However, this insistence upon engaging in works of mercy earned Wesley the accusation of pursuing works righteousness. Regarding this charge Wesley was quite clear that merciful acts are rooted in God's presence and grace in our lives.[49] Wesley actively opposed the idea that salvation by faith alone somehow cancels out the need for both works of mercy and works of piety. He went even further by stating that people who hold such a position are in danger of falling into antinomian heresy.[50] Wesley also described works of mercy as duties that must be fulfilled, and he had asserted that such duties were a necessary evidence of the follower's salvation and even promised heavenly reward.[51]

Wesley not only held together faith and works in pursuit of a middle way between opposing views but went on to intertwine the two. He accomplished this in large part by including works of mercy as means of grace, whereby practicing acts of compassion functioned as a channel of God's grace in people's lives. Wesley was careful to ground the need for this kind of work as an avenue for living out love of God and love of neighbor. This dual focus placed love at the center of Wesley's formula for living a Christian life. Christians are justified by the grace of God

48 Letter to Miss March (10 December 1777), *Letters* (Telford), 6:292–93), quoted in Maddox, "'Visit the Poor,'" in Heitzenrater, *The Poor and the People Called Methodists*, 79.

49 A discussion of this can be found in Wesley's sermon 99, "The Reward of Righteousness." See the Wesley Center Online, http://wesley.nnu.edu/john-wesley/the-sermons-of-john-wesley-1872-edition/sermon-99-the-reward-of-the-righteous/.

50 Heitzenrater, *Wesley and the People Called Methodists*, 106–7.

51 Maddox, "'Visit the Poor,'" 70. More on this topic is found in Wesley's Sermon 98, "On Visiting the Sick" at Wesley Center Online, http://wesley.nnu.edu/john-wesley/the-sermons-of-john-wesley-1872-edition/sermon-98-on-visiting-the-sick/; and in his *Journal*, 15 January 1777.

through faith; no human act can earn this free gift. However, once the believer has been justified by God's love, she must begin the process of orienting herself to this new state with the help of the Holy Spirit by living into sanctification.[52] Wesley engaged the Calvinists on this issue by pointing out that even faith is made possible by grace, and that grace is also the source of works of mercy.[53]

For Wesley, the entire process of life after having received the forgiveness of God, or justification, was a journey of living into that new relationship called sanctification. Even this process was not something followers of Christ accomplished on their own but rather was empowered by the work of God in people's lives through the Holy Spirit. Wesley was concerned to create an environment where Christians could grow in the grace and love of God, and this love of God necessarily entailed love of neighbor as well.[54] Works of piety focused upon increasing one's love of God, and works of mercy enabled the disciple to express love to the neighbor.

We have seen that works of mercy and works of piety are foundational to Wesley's ethic. Each would be incomplete without the other, though Wesley seems to prioritize works of mercy. It is possible that Wesley settled on such a priority simply out of an effort to emphasize the need for works of mercy. For people with access to wealth, the works of piety—acts of spiritual devotion, such as prayer and worship—were easier, more socially respectable, and more familiar as a well-known part of Anglican theology. It is not inconceivable that if works of mercy had been the cultural norm for religious people at the time, Wesley may have instead emphasized works of piety. While Wesley was intimately concerned with meeting the physical needs of

---

52   Heitzenrater, *Wesley and the People Called Methodists*, 320.

53   Ibid.

54   Maddox, "'Visit the Poor,'" 64. According to Maddox, modern authors writing about the need to recover a Wesleyan spirituality, such as Steve Harper and Gregory Clapper, have at times failed to express the full formative effect of acts of compassion. These scholars can overlook the crucial way that works of mercy actually shape and increase our spirituality and not simply function as a means of expressing it.

people after the example of Christ, he was ultimately concerned with meeting their spiritual needs, also after the example of Christ. However, as stated earlier in this chapter, Wesley was unwilling to separate these two practices. To care for one another's physical well-being has a spiritual benefit for the receiver as well as the giver.

If Wesley were forced to prioritize the importance of physical and spiritual healing, the spiritual healing would be emphasized because it is eternal.[55] If one simply engaged in acts of compassion without also informing the recipient of the greater possibility of grace, forgiveness, and transformation offered by God, this would be unloving and unfaithful to the calling of Christians to proclaim the gospel. This thinking, for Wesley, was rooted in the belief that when Christ inaugurated the reign of God on earth with his ministry, death, and resurrection, the care for both physical and spiritual needs were a part of Christ's work of salvation and continued to be so. The reign of God and the work of salvation cannot be relegated to exclusively spiritual matters. After the example of Christ, the Christian must work for physical and spiritual wholeness.[56]

ORGANIZING FOR MISSION

John Wesley's holistic theology was powerful but not the central component that generated such a powerful revival movement. There was little that was truly new in Wesley's theological framework, although the synthesis of theological beliefs was unusual. What set Wesley apart was his ability to create and sustain an organization to facilitate people's living out their theological beliefs in concrete and communal ways. The labeling of the followers of this movement as Methodists by its detractors was ironically appropriate; they put a method to their beliefs that

---

55 Ibid., 68–69. See also *Character of a Methodist* S16 (*Works*, 9:41) and Sermon 98, "On Visiting the Sick," I.5 and II.4; and Kenneth Collins, "The Soteriological Orientation of John Wesley's Ministry to the Poor," *Asbury Theological Journal* 50 (1995): 75–92.

56 See John Wesley, "On Working Out Our Own Salvation," at Wesley Center Online, http://wesley.nnu.edu/john-wesley/the-sermons-of-john-wesley-1872-edition/sermon-85-on-working-out-our-own-salvation/.

served as an avenue to turn such beliefs into actions, and through these actions their beliefs were strengthened.

Wesley was able to avoid the radical disconnect between theory and practice, words and actions, and intellectual assent versus inner transformation by establishing a structure that encouraged and demanded that followers live into the beliefs they professed. These practical avenues for demonstrating love of neighbor included charity schools, orphanages, medical clinics, shelters, meals, zero-interest loans, and other programs to help people meet their most basic needs and to better their condition.[57] Such programs were formed to assist and empower people according to five general categories: (1) the weak or helpless poor who needed the most basic necessities of food, shelter, and clothing; (2) the unfortunate or able poor who needed assistance in bettering their economic situation; (3) the children who needed education for mind, body, and spirit; (4) the literate but uneducated adults who could benefit from Wesley's publishing program; and (5) the poor and infirm who needed hospitals, pharmacies, and free medical advice.[58] Note that the Methodist system for assisting and empowering the poor was first and foremost to help those within the Methodist societies themselves, the majority of whom were themselves poor.[59]

In keeping with his idea of community after the example of Christ, Wesley did not encourage his wealthy patrons merely to give money to the poor but also to become personally involved with their plight. Looking once again at Wesley's correspondence with the wealthy Miss March, this point is bluntly stated. Miss March had well-grounded apprehensions about having physical contact and conversation with the poor. Wesley empathized with her objections but urged her to make such connections after the example of Christ. Wesley was not asking her to befriend the poor but to

---

57 Heitzenrater, *Wesley and the People Called Methodists*, 321.

58 Ibid., 34.

59 Ibid., 32.

> visit the poor, the widow, the sick, the fatherless in their afflic-
> tion; and this, although they should have nothing to recom-
> mend them but that they are bought with the blood of Christ.
> It is true that this is not pleasing to flesh and blood. There are
> a thousand circumstances usually attending it which shock
> the delicacy of our nature, or rather of our education. But yet
> the blessing which follows this labour of love will more than
> balance the cross (JWL, 6:208–9).[60]

The strict discipline Wesley required of members of the Methodist movement did keep the overall numbers down. To remain a member in good standing, one had to keep his or her membership ticket renewed, which required attendance at the meetings. Wesley's high expectations also helped to ensure that the Methodist membership was predomi-nantly composed of the working poor. While this makeup was not by design, there were elements of the Wesleyan revival movement that may have dissuaded the rich from joining. All of the elements in Wes-ley's ethic concerning use of wealth applied equally to rich and poor, although the wealthy perceived themselves as having more to lose monetarily than did the poor. Wesley had quite a strict definition of what wealth was that can be found in his sermon "On the Danger of Increas-ing Riches." In sum, if anyone held goods above the necessities, then one was rich. Wesley applied this definition with unyielding strictness, accus-ing those who accumulated wealth as stealing from the poor.

> Do you not know that God entrusted you with that money (all
> above what buys necessaries for your families) to feed the
> hungry, to clothe the naked, to help the stranger, the widow,
> the fatherless; and indeed, as far as it will go, to relieve the
> wants of all mankind. How can you, how dare you, defraud
> your Lord by applying it to any other purpose![61]

This kind of strict definition, coupled with Wesley's willingness to

---

60   Ibid., 252.

61   Ted Campbell, "The Image of Christ in the Poor: On the Medieval Roots of the Wesleys'
     Ministry with the Poor," in Heitzenrater, *The Poor and the People Called Methodists*,
     53–54; quoted from Sermon 131, "The Danger of Increasing Riches," S12, *Works*, 4:184.

harass donors into sharing their resources, helped to keep the number of wealthy Methodists low. Wesley's ultimate goal in the Methodist small group meetings was to have select societies where members would bring in all wealth and hold a common purse after the example of the community described in the book of Acts (2:44–45; 4:32). For Wesley, this kind of voluntary economic sharing in Christian community was the best evidence of a sanctified life. Wesley was disappointed that so few joined such societies.[62] But despite Wesley's disappointment that such economic sharing did not progress further, the Methodist movement was an incredible experiment in people worshipping God with their wealth in practical ways.

CLASSES AND BANDS

The heart of Wesley's organizational structure of the Methodist movement was the class meeting. In these small settings, Methodists were challenged to live out the gospel message. In this way Wesley not only created an avenue through which people could help one another but also a large connectional structure that allowed this Christian community to assist each other across parish, and later national, boundaries.[63] These small group meetings served as the means of challenging Christians to grow in their faith and Christian works. Such gatherings also functioned as Wesley's primary means of raising funds to sustain the many social and organizational programs of the Methodist movement.

Although the Methodists were not wealthy as a rule, as early as 1742 there was an expectation that members of the Methodist class meetings would contribute a penny a week as they were able to support special funds in the Methodist connection.[64] One lay class leader of some means, Captain Foy of Bristol, suggested that if a member could not make such a contribution, the class leader should contribute on his

---

62 Maddox, "'Visit the Poor,'" 66–67.
63 Heitzenrater, *The Poor and the People Called Methodists*, 35.
64 Ibid., 32.

or her behalf.[65] It was not, however, until much later that Wesley formalized this practice. Wesley generally kept such contributions voluntary where possible.

The Methodist revival movement grew in numbers and geographic scope, added fiscal responsibilities, expanded—resulting in building debt—and continued care of preachers' pensions and needs. An annual collection for the General Fund was established in 1761, "to which every Methodist in England" was "to contribute something."[66] It was not until 1771, however, that Wesley made this voluntary contribution into a subscription whereby every Methodist would give a penny a week or more, with the stipulation that "those who are not poor in each Society pay for those who are" (*Minutes*, 100).[67]

Although collections from societies or class meetings were the largest source of contributions to the Methodist movement, John Wesley was also not shy about going to the few Methodists of means that existed to ask them for personal donations for specific purposes. John Wesley took some delight in using the shocking term of *begging*, an illegal activity at the time, to describe his practice of soliciting wealthy supporters for special funds to help those in dire need. To give an idea of the scope of this begging, Wesley spent a week going door-to-door, asking supporters for large contributions, and raised the modern equivalent of $30,000 for the poor.[68]

EMPOWERMENT IN THE EARLY METHODIST MOVEMENT

In 1746 Wesley experimented with a different economic program of assistance: the lending stock, a sort of *micro-loan* program funded by a collection among Wesley's more affluent friends in London. Two stewards were appointed from the society to hold the fifty pounds collected for disbursement in no- or low-interest loans up to twenty shillings (one

---

65   Ibid.
66   Ibid., 31.
67   Ibid., 253.
68   Ibid., 31.

British pound) at the foundery each Tuesday morning. The micro-loans could be used for financial relief, but they could also be used to assist small business owners and managers. The loans were disbursed to members of Methodist societies, who had to pledge their repayment within three months. In the first year the lending stock assisted 250 people.[69]

John Wesley pursued a lifelong interest in medicine, demonstrated in part by his publication *Primitive Physick or, An Easy and Natural Method of Curing Most Diseases*. He published the text anonymously in 1747, eventually putting his name to it as author in 1760. Skeptical of the effectiveness of physicians, and most likely moved by those too poor to gain access to medical care, he began stocking a number of the preaching houses with medicines. Consulting with those trained in the field, in late 1746 he engaged a surgeon and an apothecary to help him to implement a regular system of dispensing medicine at the foundery each Friday. Thus, in December 1746, the foundery became a medical dispensary in accord with Wesley's intention of "giving physic to the poor,"[70] and treating those with chronic rather than acute illnesses. Following Wesley's announcement the foundery's medical dispensary soon grew to a steady monthly clientele of approximately 100 visitors at an annual cost of fewer than £120. When treatments were effective in relieving some ailments, Wesley was quick to refer to God's work in all things. Unlike the lending stock, medical dispensary services were not limited to members of the Foundery Society. Similar medical dispensaries were also generally provided at the preaching houses in Bristol and Newcastle.[71]

These experiments demonstrated Wesley's pastoral wisdom and innovation to treat both symptoms and systems of poverty, empowering many Methodists not merely to survive but to live sustainably and even flourish. As mentioned earlier, in the early decades of the Methodist

---

69   Ibid., 166.
70   Ibid.
71   Ibid., 167.

renewal movement, many of those attracted to the classes and band meetings, mostly women and youth or young adults, were considerably impoverished. In the later decades of the eighteenth century, following the movement's consolidation, those active in the movement represented in greater numbers the middle classes, possibly demonstrating a long-term effectiveness of such programs and the support of new institutional contexts.

Beginning in 1739 Wesley carried out the plan Whitefield had initially conceived of building a school for the coal-mining families of Kingswood, holding together knowledge and vital piety in the early Methodist renewal movement. The school included a large preaching hall and facilities for school administrators near Bristol. Scholars of all ages were welcome. In 1748 a new Kingswood school was opened closer to Bath, still near Bristol. The Conference deliberated on the details of the rules as well as the curriculum, which instructed children on topics from the alphabet to preparation for ministry. Subjects included reading, writing, arithmetic, French, Latin, Greek, Hebrew, rhetoric, geography, chronology, history, logic, ethics, physics, geometry, algebra, and music. Wesley wrote grammars for the English and other language courses and claimed that upon completing the Kingswood curriculum a student would be a better scholar than 90 percent of those completing degrees at Oxford and Cambridge.[72]

Wesley strove to develop a theology and structure with the ability to enable Christian disciples to live a holy and sanctified life. Although underemphasized in modern scholarship, a central part of Wesley's theology and structure was his response to the socioeconomic climate of his time through wealth sharing. The Methodist movement's highly organized structure directed followers toward the sharing of wealth by the poor and rich alike.

For Wesley, any excess wealth that a Christian possessed beyond

---

72   Ibid., 168–69.

the necessities needed for a healthy life rightly belonged to God and should be used for the relief of the poor. To fail to do so was to go against the will of God. However, to engage in wealth sharing and other works of mercy was a means or conduit of God's grace, enabling the believer to grow in the sanctified life. Wesley grounded this theology in the realities of his surrounding society and worked within the methods available to him for economic equality and true community among believers.

QUESTIONS FOR REFLECTION

1. Wesley held together works of piety (prayer, worship, singing, etc.) with works of mercy (acts of compassion to and from one's neighbors). Why is it important for Christians to hold these together in their own discipleship? What does it look like when there is an imbalance?

2. Why did the financially poor often respond to Wesley's message that Jesus died for all through grace, but that grace then motivates us to respond with grace to others, including giving financially in a sacrificial way? Is this true in your experience? Why is the good news (the gospel) better news to some than to others?

3. Discuss Wesley's assertion that one restores the gift of money back to God through the poor.

4. In his letter to Miss March, Wesley wrote, "I am concerned for you; I am sorry you should be content with lower degrees of usefulness and holiness than you are called to." Have we become content with lower degrees of usefulness and holiness than what we are called to?

5. Richard Heitzenrater referred to five categories of people on whom Wesley focused attention: the weak or helpless poor who needed the most basic necessities of food, shelter, and clothing; (2) the unfortunate or able poor who needed assistance in bettering their economic situation; (3) the children who needed education for

mind, body, and spirit; (4) the literate but uneducated adults who could benefit from Wesley's publishing program; and (5) the poor and infirm who were in need of hospitals, pharmacies, and free medical advice. Can you identify where Wesley was concerned with sustainable empowerment?

6. Does sustainable empowerment make you think differently about the mission of the church?

ZOE IN PRACTICE: SURVIVING

When Epiphanie and her colleagues first developed what was to become the ZOE empowerment program, they began with a shoestring budget to put toward program expenses but with the assumption that these children already had skills and abilities. There were things these children could do to support themselves. What they needed was not someone to provide for them but access to the first step on a pathway to provide for themselves.

The evidence for the potential of these children was easy to see. As Epiphanie witnessed, many orphans and vulnerable children get up early each day to work for others. The jobs vary, but some common ones include working in other people's fields; gathering grasses for animals; working as housekeepers; or doing other menial, low-skill jobs. Orphans and vulnerable children tend to be paid the lowest wages or are simply given a small amount of food for a day's work, and the work is often only as a day laborer. This means that there is a constant possibility that payment for a day's work can be withheld for any or no reason, with little recourse for these voiceless young people. Even relatively stable jobs, such as serving as a housekeeper, are poorly paid and sometimes carry danger. Illegal activity and prostitution are also traps these children are more likely to fall into because of their vulnerability. Epiphanie understood these children are capable of working; it is just that they are not able to benefit from their labor in a way that frees them from daily dependence on begging for work or working only for food.

ADDRESSING CHALLENGES

Orphans and vulnerable children suffer from a multitude of challenges. These range from immediate physical needs; to long-term needs to improve their lives in sustainable ways; to social, psychological needs that are often less tangible but no less critical to long-term success. What Epiphanie and her team understood was there were multifaceted challenges facing children, and any single issue had the power to hold them in poverty. For example, if a child were provided a scholarship to attend school but had malaria, he still could not attend. If someone provided her with free health care, but she was unable to buy food, the health care would be less effective. There were at least seven major obstacles holding these children in poverty. Yet when Epiphanie and her colleagues observed what services were offered, what they saw were many ministries focused narrowly on only partial causes of poverty.

The model developed by this group of Rwandan social workers is remarkably different. Instead of focusing on one difficulty at a time in isolation from all other hurdles, all the challenges holding orphans in extreme poverty are addressed in a roughly simultaneous way. This systemic approach is implemented over the course of three short years, in the context of a supportive group of peers. What they find is that, just as addressing only one area of poverty has often been ineffective, addressing multiple areas has a powerful synergy. When children acquire safe housing, they perform better in school; when they have stable sources of nutritional food, their business endeavors improve. Something seemingly insignificant, such as being clean and dressing well, changes every interpersonal interaction a young person has.

What makes ZOE work is not merely the constituent parts of the model but rather the way they are put together. Certainly the children receive interventions and training in all the areas that hold them back in daily struggles against hunger and social dislocation, but this is accomplished in the context of being part of a larger group of children with the same struggles. This group of young people goes from being a number of individual orphans all in desperate need of charity, to a group of young men and women joining together to help pull each other out of extreme poverty and sustain a better life. They are no longer charity cases but young caregivers of each other. They do receive from ZOE's program interventions, but at the same time they give to one another. Thus, their dignity, sense of purpose, and worth as human beings are preserved, while together they pull themselves up to a place of flourishing in life.

ZOE is also structured in a way that means the young participants must take ownership for the program to be effective. Of those staff who work directly with the children, there is only one staffer per one thousand children. That element of the program is why it has proven so very difficult for other organizations to replicate ZOE's results. When ZOE shares its model with other groups, there is a tremendous temptation to do more for the children. After all, they are in desperate circumstances. It takes patience and commitment to resist solving problems for the young participants.

Another discipline required for the young people to rise up as decision makers—a key element for true empowerment—is the implementing organization must sacrifice a certain amount of control over the program. It seems obvious that for a group of young people to make their own decisions, the parent organization cannot make those decisions for them. While this is an easy statement to support intellectually, it requires a large amount of self-discipline on the ground to actually implement it. Of course, relinquishing all controls would be equally foolish. If the young participants can be guided without being controlled, it can be a powerful experience for them. As a group of sixty to one hundred young people, all of whom have struggled to survive, they are extremely pragmatic in the approach to bettering their lives. As a group who has experienced extreme vulnerability, they also tend to be amazingly graceful and generous in their dealings with each other.

To pause for a moment to highlight the generosity and graciousness with which these vulnerable children work with one another is worthwhile. There are cases in each ZOE working group of orphans and vulnerable children where a young person's past physical or psychological abuse has left him or her unable to think clearly enough to understand the precepts of the program. The combined effects of malnutrition, mental illness, and disability also often play a role in providing additional challenges to young people attempting to pull themselves out of extreme poverty. In such cases, an older person in their group will often bring such an individual on as a business partner or assist him or her in learning life skills. In some cases it may be years after graduation when the traumatized young person is finally able to fully contribute to a business. We have found that the children will not allow each other to fail as long as an individual is trying to succeed.

Conversely, if someone in the group is lazy, not attending meetings, and poorly reflecting on the group through bad behavior, group members will speak with the person, visit with him or her, and attempt to assist their friend, but eventually will release that individual from the group if the behavior does not improve. This does not happen often, but the group is very serious about achieving success, and every member must be actively striving toward that goal. Another indication of this seriousness is that groups implement a system of financial fines, which they impose if members miss group meetings without sending a legitimate excuse or another representative from their siblings. In this way the group exerts positive peer pressure toward striving for success.

HOW THE PROGRAM WORKS

The basic structure of the empowerment model is a group-based, graduation model, which takes place exclusively in the village, community, or slum where the children are already living. It is a very different model for empowerment. Three quick facts about the program highlight just how distinctive the program is in practice and philosophy from many other orphan-care efforts: (1) With more than thirty-one thousand orphans and vulnerable children enrolled in the program at the end of 2016, there are no orphanages or physical structures anywhere in the world owned by ZOE. ZOE's empowerment program is not residential. (2) ZOE has roughly one staff person working directly with the young people per one thousand orphans and vulnerable children. This is not a budget limitation but the staffing point at which the empowerment program works at peak efficiency. How could this be? It is because the young people very much take the lead in their own journey out of poverty, electing their own leadership and making their own decisions. ZOE's staff are able to assist and guide, but it would be impossible for the staff to make day-to-day decisions for the young participants. (3) ZOE does not distribute any food to the children in the program. Instead ZOE stands behind the children, helping them through smaller interventions and training to be able to get the things they need for themselves.

Why is ZOE so strict on this last point of prioritizing empowerment over relief to such an extent? I (Gaston) remember attending a ZOE mission/vision trip in the first few years of the empowerment program. As is normal practice for ZOE trips, graduated young people are visited first, then those in their third year of the empowerment program, then second-year participants, and finally first-year participants. This is done to first show the hope and progress the children make, before exposing travelers to the situations participants face while living in abject poverty.

On one such trip in Rwanda, we were nearing the end of the journey for our group, and on the last day we met a young family, a fifteen-year-old girl named Claudine and her eight- and five-year-old siblings. They were so new to the program that they were only just going to their second ZOE meeting in the first few days of the program. As is normal, this young family of siblings was in difficult shape. They had not eaten in three days but had three of the smallest potatoes I had ever seen cooking on the open fire in their mud hut. This hut was in obvious disrepair, so they slept inside during the dry season and outside during the rainy season for fear that the hut might collapse upon them in their sleep. The eight-year-old girl had an open sore on her leg, which went to the bone and had little chance of healing on the subsistence diet she consumed. All their faces were gaunt and downcast, and their eyes were glazed and red. They whispered single-word answers to questions asked, in sharp contrast to the gushing remarks from bright-eyed young people with burgeoning confidence, bragging about their accomplishments in the second year of the program. It was difficult for our group and awful to behold such poverty.

The hearts of several in our group were overcome with a need to help these children. They announced that they were going back to the bus to feed these children with snacks we had brought to keep at bay even the slightest hunger pains during our journey. They knew this was in disregard of ZOE's very strict policy to give nothing away of monetary value on a ZOE trip. Even if someone on a ZOE trip consumes a bottle of water, he or she cannot give away the empty bottle. But this group of people felt they could not, as Christians, leave this desperate situation without at least leaving food behind.

Epiphanie, the founder of ZOE's empowerment model and director of the Rwanda ZOE program, physically blocked their path. She said to them, "You cannot do this." Epiphanie then pulled out her cell phone and showed them a text she had received from a similar family that morning, asking for assistance from her. Epiphanie said, "This is a family from many years ago who I worked with when we were just setting up the empowerment model. At that time I thought, *I will help this desperate family with small things and some little food, just until they are able to care for their own need, and then they can supply what they need for themselves.* But what I found is that once I offered them relief, they snapped back into the relief mentality and were never able to support themselves.

"This family you see here today, they have struggled for many years, and they will continue to struggle for the next three months before they are able to harvest their first crops and have proceeds from businesses. This is difficult to watch, but this family will be able to support themselves and will never ask me to support them."

I remember the powerful impression this made upon me. The experience of ZOE is, except in a small number of specific circumstances, that relief and empowerment do not mix. This experience accounts for the strictness of ZOE's no-relief policy. There are, however, some special circumstances where ZOE can bend its no-relief policy in the face of extreme need. If a child (or child-headed family) is in imminent danger of losing his or her life to starvation or exposure, ZOE can give the working group a special grant meant for someone in the group in extreme need. The group members, who actively visit one another and know of the needs of group members, then decide who is most in need among them and can deliver the special grant. Offering such aid through the group mitigates negative ramifications of relief. Another area where ZOE can act directly is when a young participant requires surgery or medical intervention for an illness or disability. Since one cannot be empowered to perform kidney surgery on oneself, this is an area where ZOE can provide support to secure the needed medical intervention without negatively affecting the empowerment of the children.

FINANCIAL ACCOUNTABILITY

As a young manager of a homeless shelter, I (Gaston) was approached by a member of one of our most generous support churches. He was furious. While carrying boxes up the stairs, he had dropped a twenty-dollar bill on the stairwell. When he realized what had happened sometime later, he went back to retrieve it. It was no longer there. He was demanding a search of the residents and action taken against whoever was in possession of his property, fuming that people who had received so much charity would then steal twenty dollars from those helping them.

Needless to say, we did not search residents. It is impossible to know if the money was found by a resident or volunteer, or if the supporter had dropped it elsewhere. What was clear was that dropping a twenty-dollar bill in a shelter full of desperately poor people is putting a good deal of temptation in front of them. Taking money that does not belong to you is never acceptable, but there are situations where the person putting others in a position of undue temptation, even if unintentional, shares some responsibility in the theft.

I feel the same way about supporters who send large sums of money to partners in places of desperate poverty with little by way of accounting, reporting, or measuring outcomes. While this is not an excuse for theft, it is an observation that since all of us are sinners, perhaps it is better to avoid placing undue temptation in a person's path. To send large sums of money to partners in desperately poor locations with little to no accounting is simply not responsible.

Does this mean the ZOE empowerment program remains static, without checks and balances from the U.S. staff and board? Certainly not. Sometimes organizations have a semblance of "Western guilt" and decide they will simply send money and trust their in-country partners to use it in the best possible way. For multiple reasons this approach often leads their partners to temptations to appropriate that money in a wide variety of ways. There are cases where such a stance works out very well, and there are staff who are absolutely honest, but there remain too many examples where the Western partners find the money has not been used in the manner they intended. A little more oversight, measurement, and careful procedures created and followed, and many such situations could be avoided.

ZOE has careful fiscal and quality controls. Fiscal controls are in the form of a meticulous budgeting and requisitions process, in addition to audits from highly respected firms, and quality controls are in the form of regular reporting on each group of children and spot checks from short-term trips where partners encourage the young people in the group. When either financial or reporting outliers are identified, ZOE's chief program officer, who is Kenyan, then investigates the reasons behind the situation and assists partners to take corrective action where necessary.

The U.S. staff does have critical roles to play in the ministry beyond simply fund-raising, but changes to the program itself are best done by those most knowledgeable of the program; namely, the staff and participants directly involved. This partnership between ZOE's U.S. staff and program country staff is further defined by ZOE's somewhat distinctive structure. Structures can be valuable in shaping organizational culture. To think of ZOE as a social franchise rather than a single entity gives a more accurate picture. In each country of operation, ZOE's work is carried out by an in-country partner that is a separate NGO (non-governmental organization, similar to what is referred to as a nonprofit in the United States). This in-country partner may be a separate NGO engaging in other programs besides ZOE's empowerment program, or they may be a ZOE-specific NGO. In both cases the organization has its own board and governance separate from ZOE US. While ZOE US is in weekly contact with each program, there is a large degree of autonomy with the running of the program. Partners do agree to run the program as a franchise with strict adherence to the core program ideals and methodology.

ESTABLISHING A ZOE GROUP: FIRST STEPS

When ZOE enters a community, the first activity of ZOE's indigenous staff is to speak with local leaders about orphans and vulnerable children in their community, empowerment in general, and ZOE's empowerment program. The full buy-in of community leaders, including the village chief, formal and informal government leaders, pastors, and others, is critical to the success of the program. In areas where ZOE is well established, there is often a waiting list of communities requesting ZOE to work with them. Following this engagement, group formation begins to address the basic physical level of needs.

Addressing the Lack of Food

When asked what was the worst part of how they lived before the ZOE program, children consistently respond, "A lack of food." Certainly when a child mentions this to his or her group, there is a shared understanding of what that means. A lack of food certainly means these children would often go to bed hungry, sometimes going multiple days without a meal of any kind. However, a lack of food can be measured in both quantity and quality. If they worked for food, but were paid only in potatoes or bananas, then it is possible that while their stomachs were sometimes full they were not receiving the proper nutrition they needed to stay healthy. Malnutrition as well as hunger held these children back from reaching anywhere near their potential.

How Does ZOE Address This Need?

ZOE's goal is not to supply food to these children but rather to get them to the point where they are able to grow and/or buy the food they need in order to become and remain healthy and have security that they will remain in a position to do so. This twofold focus of growing and/or buying one's own food is one of the first items addressed in the program, because if your stomach is empty it is difficult to focus on anything else. Once they achieve food stability, the young participants are able to concentrate more fully on other ways to improve their lives and form longer term goals.

To help with growing food, in all but the most urban environments, ZOE times the beginning of the program just before the coming of rainy season and growing season. In this way, working groups can be training on agricultural skills and how to raise animals early on in the program. By the time the rains arrive, participants are ready to have crops in the ground, with access to fertilizer.

Animal husbandry is important for growing food, since many ZOE programs rely on organic fertilizer to enrich the soil. Each ZOE working group will select a family to receive larger animals, which may include pigs, goats, or cows. The selected families care for the animals and share the fertilizer with other group members. Once the animal produces offspring, the family keeps the offspring and passes the mother to another group member. In this way the entire group eventually has animals of their own. Group members can also purchase animals on their own from their own business proceeds. Often these are chickens and rabbits at first, quickly building to pigs, goats, and cows.

ZOE also organizes training related to agriculture. While ZOE staff are qualified to conduct such trainings, a local farmer or ministry of agriculture official from that area provides quality training and becomes a local person outside of ZOE that the children can call upon for ongoing advice. Local ministries of agriculture have been particularly helpful partners to ZOE. ZOE participants also do an excellent job of tracking their yields and can provide valuable production data to the ministry of agriculture. Food security is a nationally important issue in each location where ZOE serves. Because of this, the government is interested in supporting citizens to fully utilize land and grow the most efficient crops.

Once training has occurred, ZOE provides each child-headed family with a hoe. After everyone's land in the group is cultivated, ZOE assists with access to seed and seedlings. In the second and third years, participants are expected to provide their own seed or save seed from previous harvests. In practice, the participants will often share land between them, especially if one child has more land than he or she can cultivate. In addition to their individual businesses, the group often also has group projects to generate additional funds. Although the specific project is at the young people's discretion, it is most often an agricultural project, because every member can participate in such an enterprise.

Even when a small amount of land is available, there are ways to produce large amounts of diversified and nutritious vegetables. One such model is a design that looks much like a wedding cake, with three or four layers of soil held in place with stakes and feed bags. In addition to being a space saver, using this method means the top "cake" layer can be watered, and the water trickles down to the other layers. Such practices help the participants augment their diet with nutritious vegetables, greatly contributing to overall health. The change in the orphans' appearance and mental functioning is palpable when they move from a situation of chronic malnutrition to a balanced diet. This is one of the many pieces of the program that works in synergy with the other aspects of the program so that the overall result is larger than the sum of the parts. Children with a healthy diet suffer less illness, improve their school performance, operate better businesses, and are better able to make plans for the future as well as work to realize them. Eyes, skin, and hair quality also improve, which makes them less identifiable as orphans from their appearance alone. While such a situation may seem cosmetic, how the children appear directly affects how they are treated and included in village events and what jobs and wages they are offered.

I was fed by African orphans. This should be a slogan on ZOE T-shirts. A common occurrence when those from the United States visit the working groups of children in the ZOE program is they are fed by these orphans and vulnerable children. This usually occurs with participants in the second and third years of the program. Although this practice is somewhat discouraged by ZOE staff, the children themselves have great pride that they are able to provide hospitality to their guests.

It is humbling to accept an ear of corn and a slightly warm Coke from children who were starving a mere twelve months before. Travelers who visit the same working group from one year to the next often comment that it is difficult to recognize the children until they look very closely. Sunken cheeks have filled out, hazy eyes are clear, smiles replace tears, and downtrodden faces now make confident eye contact. Children stand straighter and often speak of themselves as being a different person than they were just a little while before. Many of the children in ZOE's program help feed additional orphans not in the program, because now they are able to offer such kindness to others.

Addressing a Lack of Safe Shelter

A lack of shelter or inadequate shelter is a common problem among orphans and vulnerable children. The use of stucco construction means that without regular repair homes can quickly become uninhabitable. Not having adequate shelter has health implications, as well as safety repercussions for the children. They can be easily robbed or physically assaulted. Because these children are poor and voiceless, they become easy prey and have little recourse to the wrongs perpetrated against them. A particular vulnerability for orphans is that a family member may take over their property, home and/or land, with the claim that they are simply stewarding this for the minors, when in fact they have stolen this land from the children. Likewise, relatives or neighbors may take the children to live with them but use them as a source of labor and treat them as such instead of as members of the family. Of course, this is not always the situation, but such cases are all too common in the experience of orphans. If the story of Cinderella were set in modern times, it could easily be located in an African country or locations such as India.

A corollary to inadequate shelter is a lack of adequate clothing or a blanket to sleep under. All of these situations lead to exposing young people to the elements in ways that are both dangerous physically and destabilizing socially. The stigma of homelessness is a powerful force in the lives of children living in this way. Many children who come into the

ZOE program from a situation of homelessness describe themselves before ZOE as feeling more like dogs than like human children.

How ZOE Addresses Shelter

With well over thirty thousand orphans and vulnerable children enrolled in ZOE's empowerment program at the time of this book, it is often difficult to explain that ZOE is a nonresidential program. Safe, secure housing is critical to sustainable empowerment. However, as with every other part of the ZOE model, it is important that the young participants find a way to provide this housing for themselves with support from ZOE.

For those in the group in most desperate need, ZOE is able to provide housing grants to the group. These grants are typically not enough to build the entire home but to pay for the doors, windows, roof, and the advice of a contractor. The young people themselves then meet to decide who is in most need of housing. Because the children in the group share their stories and visit one another, they tend to understand each other's needs. One might think there would be a temptation for the group leadership, or more charismatic members, to lobby for their own home. But in ZOE's experience the children are concerned to help the neediest among them first. Because they have each experienced extreme poverty, and the attenuating desperation that accompanies such poverty, they tend to be extraordinarily generous with one another. Instead of devolving into a "Lord of the Flies" situation, these young people will often sacrifice themselves to help others in their groups. This all is part of the empowerment model. To be able to help another person through difficult circumstances is empowerment. To always be relegated to a charity case is deeply disempowering.

Selecting the member most in need of housing takes into account many things, including a homeless family with younger siblings with immediate threats of exposure and safety concerns. Once the *child-led* family is selected, the group assists with building materials and labor to construct the home. Often the village will assist as well. The homes are built according to the standard of the community. This sometimes means a less efficient design will be used, but the goal is not just to build the best home with the least expense but to allow the children to fit into the larger village.

Before Jonathan had joined ZOE's program in Zimbabwe, life looked hopeless. He was fourteen, taking care of two younger brothers. All of them were malnourished, dirty and dressed in rags, and hopeless. After their parents had died, grandparents took them in, but then they also died. An uncle housed them next, but his new wife turned them out when they became a strain on the family. The abandoned home they lived in had a wall and half a roof collapse, which left them partially exposed to the elements. They had land, but what meager crops they had managed to harvest the year before had been stolen since they had no way of securing a home. When these boys joined ZOE, their working group immediately identified them as a family in great need of housing. The group came together to help them build a new home where they could live securely. "We never dreamed we would have a home like this again," Jonathan shared when asked about his home. With tears in his eyes he then said how much it meant to him that his group would help him build a home. "This has changed my life, and the lives of my brothers, forever." It is a powerful piece of the program that, while Jonathan is aware that funding came from supporters of ZOE, it was his group who selected and assisted him. This focus on the group, and not ZOE, is an important piece in ZOE fading after three years but the groups continuing long after official graduation from ZOE's empowerment program.

The majority of the ZOE working groups will not receive the housing grant but rather develop a plan to save money from their businesses, purchase land, accumulate building supplies, and eventually build their own homes. The intervening steps often involve making repairs to their current homes, left to them by their parents, or having enough sustainable income to rent secure housing, until they are able to afford their own home.

To call it a house would be generous. It was just four walls made of sticks, with mud slapped on the cracks, and an old tin roof with more holes than would normally qualify it to have the name "roof." At least it provided some privacy, but little more. Still, for fifteen-year-old Perpetua, it was home. Her brother, Moses, had to move out of this hovel since it is not culturally acceptable for boys and girls to live in the same room, and that shelter offered only one room. He would sleep outside in good weather, and sometimes in a church down the street when the rains came. Renting a room was a possibility for Moses, but the difficulty was that he worked for food for himself and Perpetua. The way one rents a room with no money in Kenya is by making a deal with a landlord to have a room in exchange for labor. The usual rate is two days' labor in exchange for the room. The trouble is, when one makes a living by working each day for food or a small amount of money to buy food that day, it is a day-by-day existence. Some days there is work, and some days there may not be. Most living in this situation are never totally full, often eating the cheapest foods available, without much nutrition or variety. Some days there is just no food to be had. One experience with orphans in Africa and India that unites them in the shared horror of their past is how difficult it is to "sleep hungry." Rather than face two days each week where Moses knew there would be no food, he chose to sleep exposed to the elements.

Moses and Perpetua never shared their suffering with the group in the beginning of the program. They were ashamed of their situation, ashamed of their poverty, and ashamed to be orphans—even when in a group with other orphans. But their group members began to visit one another. Moses and Perpetua were amazed that people would care enough about them to visit them and, of course, when visiting them the group became aware of the difficult situation in which they lived. The group decided to help build a home for them. They gathered materials, and ZOE assisted them in buying a roof, doors, windows, and some cement. Very quickly the group was able to complete this home, working together. Having a secure home affects every aspect of life. Moses and Perpetua were healthier from living in a sanitary place; they could store food safely from their crops. They felt safe at night and slept better, which helped them plan their businesses and increase their prof-its. They could allow others to enter their home, which is an important cultural act of hospitality. They felt as if they were whole people and not somehow less than others. Housing is such a basic human need that when this need is met in a safe and secure manner, every other aspect of life improves.

Addressing Poor Health and a Lack of Understanding about Hygiene

Orphans often suffer from poor health due to malnutrition, starvation, and diseases associated with being both poor and vulnerable. Girls, and in some cases boys, can be subject to physical abuses leading to HIV/AIDS. Not having parents and adults able to teach basic skills in order to prevent life-threatening disease, there are many elements of extreme poverty that contribute to disease and poor health. Stunted growth and maladies from improper pre- and postnatal nutrition are common. Access to health care structures is usually severely limited. Although there is often some form of health insurance available for a nominal fee, even a nominal fee is unattainable when one is homeless and chronically hungry.

Proper health is important to every other aspect of life, yet orphans and vulnerable children often deal with constant health maladies. Those who are homeless or regularly subjected to exposure are even more likely to suffer premature death from illness. Illnesses such as diarrhea and malaria, which should be easily treatable, are often fatal for young people living in extreme poverty. Local suspicions about illness being brought about by being cursed, can further contribute to children being rejected by their community.

How ZOE Works to Improve Health and Hygiene

Right on the heels of training about how to grow food and start simple businesses, health and hygiene training is a priority. In the first year, training tends to be rudimentary and includes how to: keep one's home and one's body clean; build a proper latrine and wash hands in effective ways; boil water and cook food; store grain so it does not attract rats; sleep under a mosquito net; eat a balanced meal for good nutrition; dry dishes so that UV rays can assist in sterilizing them; use cooking pots made out of safe materials; and so forth.

This rudimentary health training in the first year of ZOE's three-year program is greatly assisted by the young people buying into national health insurance if available, growing vegetables, and caring for animals as they begin to earn income from their businesses. With their businesses and crops, they begin eating meals of sufficient quantity and quality so that their bodies are able to function properly. Having safe, secure housing; decent clothing; and blankets to sleep under all contribute to greater health.

Occasionally there is a case where a young person needs immediate surgery or medication. ZOE is careful to avoid any relief that might undermine the goal of empowerment. However, providing access to emergency surgery or health care does not interfere with empowerment in the way that distributing food, for example, interferes. Consequently, there are cases where ZOE assists children to receive the emergency care they need, and often the whole ZOE group will rally around them to assist in caring for siblings, crops, and young businesses, so they do not fall behind the rest of the group.

Esther entered ZOE's program at the age of fourteen. She had endured a very difficult life. Not only was she orphaned, but she was also born with a condition called *imperforate anus*, which basically means that she did not have an adequate anal opening. I (Gaston) first met Esther while visiting Kenya on a ZOE trip of hope. One of the U.S. travelers was particularly drawn to Esther, because her own daughter had been born with the same condition, but a relatively simple surgery had corrected the abnormality.

Esther shared with us a horrific story of difficulty and abuse. Relieving waste from her body was a constant struggle and left her incapacitated. Odor and the suspicion that she was cursed caused those around her to cast her to the side once her parents were no longer alive. One uncle, in particular, tried to kill her, feeling that her "curse" was bringing bad luck on the rest of the family. Life was a horror.

When Esther joined ZOE and shared her story, ZOE program facilitators were able to assist her to get the surgery she needed. For the first time in her life, she felt hope and the possibility that she could live a normal life. She still had much work to do to escape extreme poverty, but for the first time she felt escape was possible.

In the second and third years of ZOE's empowerment program, the training in health and hygiene increases in sophistication. In the second year young people begin learning about communicable diseases and how they spread. They are tested for HIV/AIDs, and those infected with the disease receive antiretroviral treatments. This is done in the second year in part because one must have a certain stability in life to take medication effectively. If you are starving it is unlikely that you can stick to a medical routine. By the second year, life has typically normalized enough to stay to a routine of medication.

The young people in ZOE groups often organize anti-AIDS clubs, where with music, dance, drama, and comedy they educate the wider community about the AIDS pandemic and how to avoid the disease, but also about child rights and other important community issues. Often children not from the ZOE group are also welcomed into these groups, so they are not simply stigmatized as the AIDS orphans. Many of these groups have been quite effective in educating their communities and sometimes develop a regional reputation. Additionally, hundreds of ZOE children participate in churches that provide alternative rites of passage that promise to help end the practice of female genital mutilation. In these ways the participants in ZOE groups help to enhance entire communities with the work they do.

QUESTIONS FOR REFLECTION

1. From your own experience, share a time when someone empowered you. What was it like?

2. ZOE's empowerment program was started with the gifts, skills, and potential of those being served. ZOE's relief efforts were based on the assumptions that orphans could not accomplish these things for themselves. What difference do assumptions make in shaping mission?

3. Often, American Christians are excited by ministry that is flashy and fast: ending hunger, obliterating homelessness—when the

problems need long-term solutions. How can such thinking work against multifaceted empowerment?

4. In a business relationship contracts often spell out the specific and measurable expectations of each party. Having a contract between missional partners is a discipline that is increasing in popularity but still sometimes lacks systems of accountability. How can having clear accountability systems assist in avoiding disappointment, temptation, and failed expectation? Is it somehow un-Christian to have a contract?

5. What do you think of the statement, "True empowerment should result in those empowered being able to empower others in turn"?

ZOE IN PRACTICE: THRIVING

Abraham Maslow was an American psychologist who was famous for his theory of psychological health. He created a helpful pyramid outlining a hierarchy of human needs that lead people to self-actualization. The foundation of this hierarchy, the bottom of the pyramid, represents the most fundamental of human needs: food, shelter, health, and hygiene. The hierarchy then builds on that foundation to address other needs, psychological and social, to help people become whole.

In the previous chapter we described food, security, housing, health, and hygiene — Maslow's foundational needs — as being critical to survival. In the beginning of the ZOE program, it is necessary to focus on the basic human needs because it is difficult to concentrate on anything else if our most basic needs go unaddressed. However, orphans and vulnerable children need more than survival in order to escape the cycle of extreme poverty. To thrive and succeed in life, more than physical necessities are needed. What is necessary to thrive in life includes things such as access to education and vocational training, an income-generating business, an understanding of one's rights and how to implement them, and a life plan for continued improvement that comes out of a profound sense of hope, love, and community.

ACCESS TO EDUCATION AND VOCATIONAL TRAINING

Education is a critical element to long-term success. However, ZOE has found that education, like the other interventions in ZOE's program, does not take place in isolation. It is difficult to attend school if you and your siblings are starving, you have malaria, you are homeless, you cannot afford school fees, books, or a school uniform—the list continues. If possible, however, even a basic education can help achieve success. It is challenging to run a business if you cannot add and subtract, or sign a contract because you are illiterate.

A typical situation for orphans in Africa is that they attend school sporadically. When they have some school fees, they bring them, then try to borrow other students' books, dress as well as they can, and stay in school as long as possible until they are kicked out because they are unable to pay all the school fees. They are often hungry, which affects performance, and they find themselves the source of ridicule because of their appearance. It can be incredibly difficult for a child in extreme poverty to remain in school and to thrive; and yet we see many children lift themselves over many hurdles, driven by a passion to learn and move up and forward in life. In countries such as India it can be extremely difficult to return to school after an extended absence. Each context presents its own obstacles, but attending school regularly while dealing with the myriad of challenges that extreme poverty produces is always difficult.

While education can be a catalyst for success in other areas of life, it is common for orphans and vulnerable children to have been too poor, sick, or busy earning a living to attend school for many years. Often, they have fallen so far behind that catching up in formal education is not a viable option for them, making re-enrollment difficult or impossible. In such cases, having access to vocational training, where one can learn a profitable skill, can help young people begin a successful career and earn a good income. However, when a young person is struggling with the most basic needs, such investment in skills training to ensure a better future is simply beyond reach.

How ZOE Addresses the Need for Formal Education

In the countries where ZOE operates, young people are passionate about the opportunity to go to school. Attending school is seen as one way to escape extreme poverty, so most students are highly motivated. ZOE staff work with each ZOE working group to assist members to enroll or reenroll in formal education. The younger siblings in each child-headed household are obvious candidates. In the first year of the program, ZOE assists anyone who has dropped out of school and wishes to return. ZOE helps with some portion of school fees, books, and school uniforms in the first year. ZOE staff and/or the adult mentor in each group often visit the school to help the child be readmitted. In the second year of the program, such support is less needed and so declines; and by the third year of the program, most child-headed families are able to fully fund all school expenses from their business proceeds.

It is less usual for the eldest child in a child-headed family to attend school, although this does happen. The eldest child has often been away from school the longest and feels a sense of responsibility to invest more time in a business to support the other children. In cases where the eldest children have remained in school or are academically gifted, their working group often rallies around them to assist in running businesses while the students attend school. There have even been cases where the eldest child goes off to college, and his or her working group looks after the siblings and sometimes sends support from the group. To attend college as an orphan or vulnerable child means the student has reached the top 1 or 2 percent of academic achievement in his or her country and qualifies for the limited number of government scholarships to attend college. The person's working group sees this individual academic success as the success of the entire group.

Gaston met Michael within a week of his joining the ZOE program in Kenya. As a seventeen-year-old he was head of the household for his three younger siblings. Michael did have an older sister, but she was mentally disabled and so also dependent upon Michael. This family was in difficult circumstances. Both parents had passed away some years before, and the family was obviously hungry and suffering from malnutrition. But whereas most orphans in Michael's situation would be chiefly concerned about how they would feed themselves and their siblings, Michael was concerned about school. He was academically gifted and had been at the very top of his class when he had finally had to drop out of school some months before joining the ZOE empowerment program.

The ZOE staff were a little cautious in answering his direct questions about whether ZOE would send him to school. This family was in fairly desperate shape and had many basic needs to be addressed. However, they encouraged Michael, reminding him that many things are possible with hard work. When Gaston returned to see Michael's family about eight months later, they were difficult to recognize. Michael's next oldest sister was particularly hard to recognize as she spoke for the family. Her once-gaunt face had filled out; and cloudy, downcast eyes had given way to a confident air of hope. She spoke about returning to school, and her businesses were enough to cover school fees for herself, her younger siblings, and her older brother. Her ZOE working group was also assisting Michael to purchase the books he needed as he continued his education and prepared for college.

Vocational Training

Many orphans and vulnerable children are relegated to low-skill wages. Even with such manual labor, they are often paid less than other laborers. Some of this has to do with the fact that they are orphans in desperate poverty and therefore will accept lower wages. Other reasons have to do with what they can physically accomplish because of their age and physical health. There are also situations where semiskilled labor is paid on different scales according to whether or not one has access to his or her own tools. For example, a carpenter with her own tools is paid at a different scale than a carpenter of the same skill level without tools. Because of the desperation of circumstances, many children are relegated to working for food or very meager pay. Not only does such subsistence work keep them completely dependent upon their employer for day-to-day survival; it also means they have no recourse if an employer refuses to pay them for their labor. Working for food, or working for a room or as a house girl, can be almost indistinguishable from slavery. In many cases, especially in India, ZOE girls were caught up in formal or informal child trafficking situations before the ZOE program. Sex work can offer survival at one level, but only temporarily and at tremendous costs. When working with children, even if there is tacit assent to such work, it is never voluntary.

How ZOE Addresses Vocational Training

In cases where a young person has been away from school for five or more years, and has three or four siblings to support, formal education is sometimes not a viable option. In such situations ZOE offers vocational training. This is a way to increase one's earning potential without formal education. ZOE does not prescribe which businesses participants should engage in. If a business requires vocational skill, the young person wanting vocational training will make a proposal to his or her group, and the group will decide how to use the limited resources it has for investing in that individual's vocational training. Upon graduation from vocational training, the group will also provide the graduate a start-up kit so the young person can immediately begin his or her trade. Different businesses have different costs and require different training. Skills such as hairdressing or barbering require shorter training than does welding or auto mechanics, and the start-up kits for the former trade are less expensive than for the latter two. In deciding who is able to begin vocational training first, groups take into consideration many factors, such as the passion and preparation of those applying for funding. By the third year most participants who want such training are able to have it.

During the first weeks of the ZOE program, staff will survey the group to see if anyone in the group already possesses vocational skills. It may be that a young woman has worked as an assistant for a hairdresser for some years, and has gleaned the necessary hairdressing skills, but lacks the resources to start her own business. In such cases ZOE can make a business start-up kit and small grant immediately available, and the young person can open her business quickly. This kind of quick start also acts as encouragement to other group members, who see how a vocational skill translates into a higher income with less physically demanding work.

Vocational training is a viable alternative to continued formal education, and in some cases can be preferable. Many foreign-funded programs are focused on providing maximum educational opportunities, and certainly education is important. However, in countries where the unemployment rate may be 70 percent or higher, even achieving a bachelor or master's degree does not guarantee employment. To make an obvious but pertinent point, you cannot eat a diploma. Formal education must be balanced with life skills so that the end result is a young person who is self-sufficient. Where both are possible, that is an ideal situation, which ZOE strives to achieve. However, life skills are the key component for becoming self-sufficient in three years.

In many cases with ZOE, the eldest child in a family will not go to college, but his or her children will have that option. I (Gaston) am reminded of my own family history, which many in the United States share. My grandfather dropped out of school in the eighth grade, even though he was an excellent student. He was needed to assist the family on the farm. He worked hard to make a better life for his family; both of his sons acquired master's degrees, and one earned a doctorate. Their children in turn all had the option of pursuing as much education as they felt was needed to achieve their goals. ZOE focuses on creating this kind of generational change in the lives of its participants.

When ZOE working groups approve group members for vocational training, the typical next step is for the apprentice to find a mentor/trainer in his or her own community. While it is sometimes necessary to attend a vocational school for certain activities, ZOE has found that for the orphans it is often preferable to have a traditional apprenticeship. This is partly because vocational schools sometimes require a certain level of formal education, which ZOE participants may or may not possess. An advantage to having a mentor in the community, rather than attending a vocational school elsewhere, is that the mentor can act as another local connection for the young person. This contact person can be part teacher, part adult mentor, part business colleague, and part friend. For young people still struggling with social dislocation, having such relationships greatly increases their chances of long-term success.

A trend that is especially prevalent in mature ZOE programs is that a majority of apprenticeships are conducted by other ZOE orphans further along in the program, or even members in the same working group training other group members who enter the vocation after them. While ZOE encourages such apprenticeships to be paid, often the skilled orphan will do this free of charge or for a greatly reduced rate as a way of paying forward what he or she has received. Another benefit to having one orphan train another is that these young people understand their distinctive situation far better than someone who has not had their experience. They tend to have more patience with an apprentice who must still care for younger siblings or provide financially for others, or who may have self-esteem issues from past traumas. Another young person who shares that experience will intimately understand some of the barriers unique to orphans.

Donata had worked in a beauty salon for years, sweeping and assisting with small tasks. Her pay was barely enough to survive, but she was fascinated by the work. Her dream was to have her own shop, but that seemed a dream without possibility. Whenever needed, she assisted with hair and was constantly watching how the work was done. All of her friends received free hairstyles as she practiced in her limited free time. Donata worked several other menial jobs to make sure her two younger siblings had food and could usually attend school. At age fifteen she heard about ZOE coming to her village. When she heard the staff talk about empowerment, she was intrigued. Another orphan farther along in the program shared that her group had helped her with vocational training, a start-up kit, and some money to rent a shop. Donata could not believe what she was hearing, and her long-concealed dream seemed a bit closer. Donata was surprised when, a month into the program, her group was asked if anyone had a vocational skill. She was hesitant at first but raised her hand. Her heart swelled with excitement and nervousness when her group agreed to give her a start-up kit and help her rent a shop.

Donata had dreamed of this for years and worked day and night to start her shop. Her group helped her spread the word, and soon she had a thriving business. A year later Donata was a seasoned business-woman and had trained an additional four orphans from her group and employed two additional orphans who were in a situation similar to Donata's before ZOE.

EARNING AN INCOME

As previously discussed, it is extremely difficult for orphans and vulnerable children to earn a living. They are hungry and often seen as a nuisance in their village. They beg for food or for work, but most people around them have little extra to share. The jobs they can find are ones no one else wants, such as carrying water, shoveling out animal sheds, cutting grasses for feed, working on other people's farms, or serving as house help. In most cases they are paid either with food or very low wages, and work is sporadic. If they happen to work all day but are refused payment, they have little recourse. It is a miserable and precarious way to live, and many children's stomachs are rarely ever completely full, making strenuous work even more of a challenge.

How ZOE Helps Participants Start Businesses

It is important to have some way to purchase food and other basic needs for a person and his or her siblings to live. To begin a business, an orphan or vulnerable child needs to be able to accomplish several things. First there must be a way to receive education on how business works, including evaluating a market, profit margins, and risk. These topics need not be complicated but do need to be fully understood. Training on not only developing a business plan but also on financial management is fundamental to business success. ZOE begins very early in the program to train the young people on how to develop a business plan. Sometimes such training is conducted by the ZOE staff, but often local successful businesspeople or government officials in charge of encouraging business development volunteer to conduct training with the young people. This is coupled with a goodly amount of peer-to-peer discussion inside the working group, with younger working groups looking at what has been successful for more mature working groups.

After a young person understands these concepts and develops a plan, then access to capital to begin a business must be secured. In the first year of ZOE's program, the working group is given a lump sum of money—a micro-grant—to be used for small grants to individual group members. The reason ZOE begins with a micro-grant instead of a loan is that these young participants would likely not take a loan. They would not qualify for traditional micro-lending programs and have no assets to put against a loan. Starting with a grant allows these children to begin with businesses even before they are fully convinced they can succeed.

Once a group receives their grant, the group treasurer is excited to have something to do, and he or she opens a group bank account— usually with seventy-plus other children—and puts the money in the bank, keeping careful records. These records are also monitored by the group, with reports given each week. The children are trained on how to manage money, operate a business, and create a business plan. Then each child-led family comes up with a business proposal. They bring this proposal to the group meeting; the group discusses it, gives constructive feedback, and if it is viable, approves the grant. The child-led family receiving the grant then feels that this is money their group has given to them. They understand the money came from donors far away, of course, but it is received through their group.

The young people work hard to make their businesses succeed. There is quite a bit of cooperation and sharing of knowledge between the children. At their weekly meeting, and as they meet informally throughout the week, they share ideas, challenges, and successes for the upbuilding of everyone.

The initial businesses are often quite rudimentary. The young people are still struggling with poverty and just learning how business works, so simple may be better. Examples of businesses include buying and boiling eggs, and then selling the boiled eggs, or making and selling charcoal. Growing crops and raising animals also make for good initial business ideas. Not every young person succeeds immediately, but they all learn about the concepts of running a successful business.

For example, say that Pierre is a fourteen-year-old boy who decides that with part of his initial grant of about thirty dollars, he will purchase five chicks, then fatten them up and sell them as full-grown chickens. Since ZOE does not distribute food, and this occurs in the first month of the program, it may be that Pierre is still hungry. In such a situation, with five fat chickens under his care, it is not inconceivable that he may eat a chicken, and the first may taste so good that the other four follow. That is not ideal for Pierre, but it is built into the ZOE model that some of the young people will not succeed at their first attempt. However, another person in Pierre's group, sixteen-year-old Sofia, has a plan to make soap and sell it in the local market. Because you cannot eat soap, Sofia sells her soap and succeeds in making a profit. Each week the young people share their successes and failures, and they begin to understand how business works and how business discipline helps them to be more successful. There is a powerful and positive peer pressure among the group, with friendly competition surrounding who can be the most successful. They also take care to frequent each other's businesses. Reegan Kaberia, ZOE chief program officer (introduced earlier), encourages groups to keep a dollar (or shilling, rupee, quetzal, etc.) in the group as much as possible. "It should touch five hands in the group before leaving the group," Reegan urges. In this way there is a built-in market, which is critical to helping fledgling businesses begin to make a profit. Local villagers will also encourage the young people in their businesses.

At the same time group members are conducting individual businesses, they also engage in at least one group income-generating project. This could be agricultural, raising chickens, pigs, or goats, or any other business they feel will be successful that can involve the entire group. For the individuals whose initial businesses failed, income from this group activity provides enough to get them through to the next grant cycle. It also provides extra income to the group account, which continues to build over the three years in the ZOE program, and which the group continues to manage past graduation. As mentioned earlier, each component of the ZOE program operates in synergy with the rest. The group activity tends to be a time when these young people share their stories with one another. It is a source of building community, healing from social dislocation, asking advice of one another, and working together to accomplish a task.

In the second and third years of the program, businesses operate on a much different level. The young people now understand how business works and are more sophisticated in their business plans. In these latter years ZOE provides money to be distributed by the group as a loan instead of a grant. ZOE does not receive these loans back; rather, they stay with the group in perpetuity. ZOE has now traced groups five, six, and seven years past graduation, and they continue meeting weekly and using this revolving capital to grow businesses, and even to help additional orphans.

The same general cycle is followed in the second and third years, but at a higher level. Money is given to the group, and the treasurer puts it in the group bank account. More in-depth business training occurs, and more comprehensive business proposals are presented to the group. The group meets together to decide what interest rate to charge each other and then makes loans as business proposals are approved. The young participants find a much higher rate of success in these second and third cycles. They pay back their original loans with interest to the group fund. Once their businesses are growing, they have enough profits to satisfy their own needs and to further invest to build their businesses and start new ones.

By the third year in the program, a child-led family will have two or three diversified businesses. Such diversification is helpful for long-term success, employing the old example of selling both umbrellas and ice cream; whether the weather is sunny or rainy, one can make a profit. Young people who diversify their business portfolios are able to weather droughts or changes in markets. Also, because ZOE participants are taught the skills needed to start a business, if there is some disaster, such as a war or famine, these young people have the resilience to build themselves up once again.

By the third year in the program, many ZOE participants have employees of their own, who operate one business while the owner is tending to other businesses. In the vast majority of cases ZOE participants will hire other orphans or other vulnerable members of their society as employees as a way to assist them.

An orphan in Kenya, named Patrick, illustrates this point. When Gaston first met Patrick, he was standing in the middle of his huge tree nursery, which was his business, and grinning from ear to ear. Before Gaston stood an eighteen-year-old young man with all the promise and hope in his eyes that anyone could wish for his or her child. But Patrick's life was not always this way. When Patrick was just fifteen, and the oldest of six siblings, tragedy struck. His father died, leaving behind his wife, who developed a mental illness, and six children ages three to fifteen. As the oldest child, Patrick became the family's sole provider.

Asked how he survived, he said it was difficult. He would just move around, begging for work. He would work from sunup to sundown and make a little less than forty cents a day. It was not enough to feed a family of seven. They would eat once a day, but not a real meal, and never enough to not feel hungry. They lived in a hovel, which was beginning to edge into disrepair. For seven years they survived like this. Then Patrick heard about an orphan program coming to his village, called ZOE.

The brilliant smile returned as he recalled how he joined his ZOE working group and immediately felt accepted. For the first time, Patrick had hope that tomorrow could be better than today. That hope began to take shape when his group sent him for vocational training on how to germinate trees—which resulted in Patrick operating a large tree nursery, where he grew trees from seedlings meant to be used in planting hedges. As the business grew, Patrick added seventeen employees to assist with planting and cultivating the trees. Asked who he employed, since so many ZOE orphans employ other orphans, Patrick said he employed widows in his community. He went on to explain that widows in his community found it hard to find work and often had children for whom they had to provide. By employing widows and offering flexible hours, he found he could be a big assistance to them. There is a deep beauty in this idea of a vulnerable orphan becoming a caregiver and empowering widows in his community.

In empowering orphans and vulnerable children to conduct business, one also can see unintended consequences of *large-scale aid*. Here is an example. As a group business project, a ZOE working group of orphans and vulnerable children in Malawi purchased corn at harvest, when the supplies were high and prices low. They rented a location to store the grain and had researched the market to make sure their investment was well placed.

Such an investment would traditionally be low risk and relatively high reward. However, Malawi experienced a drought that year and reaped lower-than-usual harvests. The young people in the ZOE group had used drought-resistant crops and thus harvested more than the average. Normally a low-harvest situation would be good for their business of holding harvested grain until prices rose. However, before the peak time to sell corn came, the market was flooded with outside food aid in the form of corn. The market plunged and the orphans lost most of their investment.

This is one example of why aid and relief efforts can have many unintended consequences. It is important to give aid in such a way that it does not undercut the local economies. If such economies are undercut, it can amplify the problem instead of addressing it. For example, if corn is regularly sent to Malawi free of charge, then farmers stop growing corn, or any crop where there is a high risk of losing money. In time the country becomes more dependent upon the outside aid instead of less dependent. This cycle of aid and growing dependencies on that aid is a *well-established* phenomenon.

KNOWING AND ADVOCATING FOR CHILDREN'S RIGHTS

A major area needed for young people to thrive is education on the rights of the child, which are internationally recognized. The difficulty for many orphans and vulnerable children is they are either unaware of these rights or their voices are not heard when they call for their rights to be honored. Orphans need to know their rights and how to receive them. They also need to be placed socially so that they have support structures that help to amplify their voices. This can take the form of a respected advocate to whom people in power will listen. Being a part of a larger group also helps protect its members. Without such measures, any success an orphan has can simply be taken from that child; he or she can be denied the right to go to school, utilized as slave labor, trafficked, beaten, and abused. Another large problem for orphans is that the ancestral land their parents left for them can be taken over by relatives or others. If the child has no voice and does not understand his or her rights, that child has no recourse in such a situation.

How ZOE Helps Young People Advocate for Their Rights

Child-rights training is conducted as early as possible in the ZOE program. While ZOE staff are able to conduct this training, they most often recruit the government official or local person in charge of enforcing such rights to conduct the training. This allows the children to develop a relationship with the person in charge of this area and for that official to understand what these children are trying to accomplish. Such relationships are almost as important as knowledge in achieving one's rights. The young participants in a ZOE working group also benefit from the fact there are sixty to one hundred of them in the group. Having a large group amplifies voices.

An orphan in Kenya, named Sarah, illustrates the difficulty in receiving rights as a vulnerable child. At age twelve Sarah was left orphaned, with a younger brother to care for. Instead of family being a source of support to her, her uncle took the opportunity to rob her of her land. Sarah's parents had left their children with a decent home and five acres of land, which is a large amount in Kenya. After the parents' death, however, her uncle claimed stewardship of the land, saying that Sarah was too young to utilize it. The uncle shared no proceeds of the land with Sarah but used it for his own purposes. Sarah went to the village chief to plead her case but was not heard by him. After all, it was a dispute between a teenage orphan and a grown man with land in the village.

At fourteen Sarah joined a ZOE group. She had experienced so much suffering in her young life that being around people who accepted and assisted her was like a dream. She now had a child after having been forced into a situation for food to feed her brother and herself, and her desperation had only increased. During the child-rights training she shared her story with her group. The group wanted to assist Sarah, so all seventy-nine of them went to the village elder. Seventy-seven of them held vigil outside while the chairperson and Sarah went in and spoke with the village chief. She emerged with rights over her land.

Sarah's working group helped her cultivate her land, which she shared with them as one of the group businesses. After a few short years in the program, Sarah had opened a tailoring shop and had a working farm and a large herd of more than twelve goats. Once hungry, she now has plentiful food stored for her and her family. She is also an advocate for the rights of other children.

DEVELOPING A LIFE PLAN

All of us, but orphans and vulnerable children in particular, need a life plan. To have articulated one's goals and the steps needed to achieve them is a powerful tool in moving forward in life. Such a plan needs to be realistic. Having sage advice from both mentor figures, people experienced in specific areas, and loving peers all play a role in honing one's vision for the future. The verse "Where there is no vision the people perish" is most certainly true for those most vulnerable who have additional hurdles to success. Unfortunately, everything in the life of a child in extreme vulnerability conspires against making plans for the future. When a child goes to bed hungry each night, it is difficult to think about more than from where the next meal is coming. Malnutrition, coupled with the physical and psychological abuse from which many orphans suffer, leaves one's brain foggy and makes strategic thinking difficult. Because of social shunning that poverty also brings, there are also no adults surrounding them from whom they can ask advice. They end up living from day to day, always living on the edge of survival.

How ZOE Helps Young People Develop a Life Plan

Establishing both hope that tomorrow can be better than today and a plan to achieve that better life is addressed at the very beginning of the ZOE program. Usually in the third meeting of their working group, after hearing about how the empowerment model works and electing officers, the young people are asked to think about their individual dreams for life.

The young people are gathered together and asked to close their eyes and imagine where they would like their life to be in two years' time, in five years, and in ten years. Staff then distribute poster paper to each child, divided into quadrants with a fifth section carved into the bottom. In the first quadrant the young people are asked to draw pictures in response to the question, "What makes you sad?" The pictures the children draw are often of people beating children or some other kind of abuse. This is a helpful tool to ZOE's staff because it gives them an overall picture of the kinds of things these children have struggled with or have experienced. It also helps the children articulate their pain in a nonthreatening way.

In the second quadrant the young people are asked to draw pictures in response to the question, "What makes you happy?" In the majority of cases, this is a depiction of food. When you are hungry, it is food that makes you happy. One young girl drew a flower because flowers make her happy.

In the third quadrant the young people are asked to draw pictures responding the question, "As you walk around your community, what is it that you do not like?" This is often answered with depictions of drunkenness, prostitution, witchcraft, or other behaviors the children encounter in their village.

In the final quadrant the children draw pictures of their individual dreams to answer the question, "What is your dream for the future?" ZOE staff guide the young participants to help them envision goals that are realistic and practical. It does not help anyone to draw a picture of a jet plane and say he wants to be an airline pilot by next year. It is better to focus on what can be achieved in the next year or two. A typical dream would include a picture of a house, a cow, and a bicycle—all things that represent success to many orphans.

Finally, there is a triangle carved into the bottom two quadrants to write out the children's "life principles." Their responses answer the question, "What are the things you must do each day to move from where you are now to where you want to be?" In the first year these are usually very simple, such as "Follow the program" and "Listen to the ZOE staff." By the third year they are often verses of Scripture or business philosophy.

Some of the young people will volunteer to share their dreams with the group. All are encouraged to take these and hang them in their homes or businesses where they can see them every day. As parts of their dreams are achieved, they check them off. Roughly annually, the young people draw new dream charts to continue to inspire them.

In addition to their individual dreams, participants in ZOE's empowerment program, particularly in their second and third years, can describe goals for their businesses and progress on saving toward a house or animal or tools to help earn more income. They can share with you dreams for their siblings, qualities they are looking for in a spouse, and how they hope to help others as they themselves have been helped. Having a life plan is tremendously empowering.

HOPE FOR A BETTER TOMORROW

Modern poverty studies often account for the phenomenon that poverty is not in its essence a lack of wealth, but it is a lack of hope. In working with orphans and vulnerable children—or any vulnerable group, for that matter—a sense of hope and possibility must first be present before any lasting life improvements can materialize. The reason for this is simple. If one does not have hope that tomorrow can be better, then why work for a better tomorrow? Hope is fundamental to developing a life plan and sacrificing to achieve that life plan.

Gaston once worked for a local Habitat for Humanity affiliate. Habitat for Humanity was an enormous opportunity for a homeowner, especially when interest rates were high. The homeowner put his or her own sweat equity into building a home, and many people and resources were focused on providing a quality home for that person, with a monthly mortgage that was affordable. The default rate for homeowners at this affiliate was extraordinarily low, but default still meant that the homeowner would lose the home. In the handful of cases where a default occurred, a pattern arose. Quite often the homeowner would have a large SUV in the driveway with an equally impressive monthly payment, many times what the home payment was. There would be furniture and electronics also on lease in the home, in what seemed a flagrant disregard for financial planning, even though financial training was part of the vetting process for Habitat homeownership.

The reaction from many donors and volunteers was one of shock that a homeowner would throw away such a wonderful long-term asset to enjoy the temporary trappings of a better lifestyle. However, with minimal inquiring the underlying cause in many cases was discovered: a lack of hope. Certainly not for all, but for some people who had grown up in a generational cycle of poverty, the promise of breaking out of that cycle seemed unimaginable. An enjoy-it-while-you-can mentality had set in. If a person's entire experience of anything good was that you should take full advantage because no matter what you did it would either disappear or be taken from you, then the concept of sacrificing to build a better financial life made little sense. Hope is a fundamental need. For many who had high expectations of life as part of their upbringing, it may be difficult to enter into a hopeless reality. The cycle of poverty has many tools to hold people in its clutches, and hopelessness is chief among them.

How ZOE Addresses Hope

The individual components of ZOE's program are important, but the result is much greater than the sum of its parts. ZOE is not primarily about implementing a series of interventions in the lives of children but about building children. Hope is a primary part of building a child. From the first meeting, ZOE begins working to instill this sense of hope. The staff speak about empowerment and the possibility that tomorrow can be better than today. They share with the children that God loves them and will be with them. Children farther along in the program share their success and words of encouragement; and then the children in the group share their own stories with one another. All of this sharing sets in the young people's minds the possibility that life can get better.

ZOE begins the program with some immediate wins for the children through growing crops, receiving animals, and starting businesses. Seeing their own success and the success of others in their group further undergirds their hope. In the first year of the program, there are many small victories, which contribute to the overall effect of life improving.

SOCIAL DISLOCATION

After hope, another powerful force holding orphans and extremely vulnerable children in a cycle of poverty is social dislocation. Orphans in areas of extreme poverty are often sick; dirty; dressed in tattered, dingy clothing; begging; and they may even steal food if they or their siblings are starving. Others begin to shun them, the way beggars are shunned. In areas where so many are struggling to survive, engaging with hundreds of begging children can be overwhelming. The social structures that may have once facilitated these children to be taken in by a neighbor or relative have been overwhelmed. These children are seen increasingly as a problem, even a pariah, on the larger community and pushed off to the side.

At the same time the orphans themselves often begin to self-segregate. They understand they are not dressed appropriately, nor are they clean, and they are often exhausted and hungry. It is not unusual for them to be taunted or even beaten by others, so it is easier just to keep to themselves in many instances, and only interact with others when driven by necessity. This includes community gatherings, such as attending church. One young person described his most vulnerable time when he was homeless and staying alive by eating whatever was left over from a pig trough that he was hired to clean. "I felt more like a dog than a human child." This feeling of being somehow subhuman, cursed by God, and not worthy of love is common.

Orphans and other vulnerable children also feel alone in their suffering. Even though there may be hundreds of such children in a small area, they often feel alone, as if they are the only ones who suffer as they do. A common complaint of children from these vulnerable years is, "There was no one who would visit me." When asked to describe what life was like before they became empowered, this complaint is almost as common as memories of "sleeping hungry." This speaks to how powerful social dislocation is in these children's experiences.

How ZOE Addresses Social Dislocation

What is necessary to combat this sense of isolation and unworthiness is not a simple answer, but there are several distinct factors that contribute to healing this situation. Being a part of a loving, supportive group of peers who have shared this sense of suffering themselves is a primary way for young people who have suffered to feel included. The very beginning of ZOE's program is for the young participants to form mutually supportive working groups of sixty to one hundred children each. The groups elect leadership with a great amount of festivity for all who run for office. They set up official rules and a meeting schedule. For these children to belong to such a group is in itself a powerful countermeasure to the social dislocation and isolation they previously felt. Because the children in the group share so many things in common, each member feels understood by the other children in the group. They have all slept hungry, all been abused, all felt less than human; now they have a chance not only to help themselves but also to help one another. This aspect of helping others is fundamental to their empowerment. To have to receive is disempowering, but to be able to give transforms a person from a charity case to a young caregiver.

Of course, having their own money, and the things money can buy, also helps these young people to fit into their community. To be clean and well-dressed, especially if one has looked like a beggar for a significant part of his or her life, is a powerful change. It means when people look at such an individual, they see a talented, successful young person and not a community problem. This goes well beyond the superficial. It is the difference between people speaking to these young people when passing by, or ignoring them; between receiving a fair wage for work, or being paid in food or little to no money; between feeling they can go to church or community events, or keeping to oneself; and between having people listen to them when they have a complaint or idea, or watching people ignore them. The way they look and dress changes a staggering number of small interactions that take place each day. The cumulative effect of these changes has a powerful connection to self-esteem and social positioning. ZOE spends a good deal of time on health and hygiene, washing clothes, and personal grooming. The children's outer appearance begins to reflect the inner change they are undergoing.

MENTORSHIP

The importance of having mentors in one's life is again an aspect all people share, but one which orphans and very vulnerable children feel more acutely. Mentorship can emanate from a variety of places; but while they are struggling in poverty, these young people often have few adult role models. Too often the adults in their community who do engage them do so only to exploit them for labor or other, more insidious purposes. The young person begins to avoid social interactions for fear of being harmed by them.

How ZOE Addresses Mentorship

Each ZOE working group selects a group mentor, some adult in the community whom the children see as a supporter and advocate. The ZOE staff then verify this person in the community to ensure he or she has the best interest of the children as a primary goal. This volunteer position fully participates in every aspect of the program. These adults become the mentors the children can trust for advice and assistance. A good adult mentor contributes in powerful ways to the children's success.

A successful community leader can mentor children in ways that immediately give the young people social legitimacy. When a village chief or important person in the community takes the time to encourage and share information with children who have felt isolated, it lifts them in a number of ways.

Other than the official adult mentor for the working group, many other adults in the community assist the group with training. These adults form another circle of people in the community who want to see the young people succeed. Many young people attend vocational training as an apprenticeship and form mentoring relationships with the craftsperson who conducted their training. Even inside the group some of the older children will mentor the younger ones. This can be a powerful force for lifting up the entire group.

It was hard to see John Claude when he first entered the program. He spoke of losing his mother after caring for her as she wasted away. He would not believe she was gone until neighbors came in and took her body away. He was left as a twelve-year-old boy with two sisters, ages six and eight. The whole family was devastated by their grief.

John Claude was invited into a ZOE group when he was fourteen. However, he lived from day to day, cutting grasses to feed neighbors' animals, and kept missing his group meeting because he had to work to feed himself and his sisters.

The chairperson of his ZOE working group visited him and came to understand his reasons for not attending the meetings. The chairperson then shared John Claude's difficulty with the group, and they formed a plan to assist him. He had a large plot of land, but he was unable to plant it by himself. So, the group met at his home the next week, and everyone together cultivated and planted his field. This so impressed John Claude that he started coming to meetings, and his life began to improve. However, life for his sisters was still difficult. They were so traumatized from the loss of their mother that they were listless, depressed, and dirty.

Mary was an eighteen-year-old young woman in the working group. She understood that John Claude found it difficult to help his sisters learn how to groom themselves, bathe, and deal with their grief and depression. So, Mary would stop at their house each day, talking with them and teaching them how to care for themselves, in addition to caring for her own siblings. On Sunday she would take them to church. She helped them become young women.

The change in their lives over a short twelve-month period was dramatic. They began to talk and to manage businesses. They dressed well and kept themselves clean. Mary's attention to them helped them emerge from the darkness into a brighter world.

FAITH AND SPIRITUAL DEVELOPMENT

So often orphans and vulnerable children struggle with thinking about God. Many orphans will say either that they cannot believe that God exists, or that they feel that God does exist but God must hate them, because their lives are such a tragedy. In other cases the children feel they do not deserve God's love, or they struggle to believe that God, or anyone else, could ever love them.

Historically, there have been too many cases where Christian missionaries have gone to places of extreme poverty to offer relief. When those who are desperately poor discover that the people giving them things really want them to convert, or that conversion will get them more assistance, the conversion rate can be quite high. Yet, when the Christian missionary leaves, it is discovered that perhaps many such conversions were more pragmatic than spiritual. This is not to say that there are not people who come to true faith through such an experience, but this is a bit anemic as an evangelistic technique.

How ZOE Addresses Faith and Spiritual Development

ZOE is religiously nonrestrictive in whom is served, and noncoercive in sharing the Christian faith with participants. ZOE's evangelism is highly effective but also very gentle. If a Muslim or Hindu child joins a ZOE working group, and then graduates as a Muslim or Hindu, ZOE does not see that as a failure: the participant has both seen and heard the gospel message, in powerful ways, during his or her three years in the program. Conversion must come from God. In the meantime, the ZOE staff and mentors share their faith, and the children are amazed that people who did not even know them would give of their resources to help them. That is the kind of love in action that is incredibly compelling for them.

Where it is culturally appropriate, ZOE staff walk the children through the Lord's Prayer in their first meeting. They spend time discussing what it means for an orphan to call God "Father." They are assured that God does love them, and many children respond to this message. In most cases group meetings start in prayer, and often the groups will elect a chaplain to lead their group worship. ZOE also encourages young participants to attend church, where many come to take leadership roles. The ZOE children have a powerful testimony about God's love in action. They also begin putting Christian principles into action with how they deal with one another and others outside of their community.

There are some who feel ZOE should not address a desire that children should know the love of God in Christ at all. Often such feelings stem from more traditional practices by missionaries that, although too complicated to parse in this work, were sometimes overly coercive in their approach. ZOE both shares and shows the gospel with these children, while taking great care to preserve their own choice and never treating a child as anything less than a full member of the group, regardless of religious belief. For others this approach is not forceful enough. However, an important point for ZOE's evangelism is that other than participants in India, almost every child in ZOE's program has been abused or neglected by a Christian. Simply showing up and saying, "Jesus loves you" may not be enough. Children must see the gospel in action as well as hearing about God's love for them, and without coercion. In such a situation God's power is evident.

A working group of orphans in Rwanda decided to have a goat

herd as a group project to raise money. They bought about ten goats and cared for them. As it turned out, the goats liked each other, and they ended up with many more goats than they were expecting. So, they met to decide what to do with their abundance. At the same time they were reading about forgiveness in the Bible and discussing what this meant for them. The group decided to put their faith into action.

This group of orphans and vulnerable children had been particularly abused by members of their village when they were vulnerable. They certainly had much to forgive. They decided to identify twelve families in their village and presented each of them with a goat as an act of Christian reconciliation.

The power of young people understanding that they are not beyond the love of God in Christ, but are being trusted to make such a decision on their own, is a powerful form of evangelism. The depth and power of the way these young people respond to the love of God is one of the areas where they can give back to American churches who support them financially. These children are truly rich in spirit, and they understand the redemptive power of God and what it means to truly depend on God for their daily bread.

QUESTIONS FOR REFLECTION

1. While many ZOE participants do go to college, the majority do not. ZOE's purpose is to create generational change so the children of participants will be able to go to college and have other choices in life. Often, we put *ill-fitting* measures of success, such as a college degree, electricity, or home ownership, on those we "serve." While wonderful, these may not be the same measures of success participants in a program hold. How should a mission define what success looks like?

2. When a ZOE participant or graduate offers to train another child pro bono, give a meal to a visiting supporter, or adopt a child, why is it important to accept that person's gift rather than try and convince him or her otherwise?

3. In ZOE's program both successes and failures help teach the individual participants and the entire group. How many communities do we have where it is safe for us to both succeed and fail?

4. Why is it so critical to ZOE's success that the young participants make their own decisions? When people first hear of the model, many are deeply skeptical of having one direct staff person per thousand orphans; and they are outright scandalized by the thought of not giving food to hungry children. Why are these pieces so critical to the success of ZOE's program?

FROM GLOBAL TO LOCAL

There is often a rift between global and local as areas of charitable focus, as if one must choose between the two. This is unfortunate in that the two should work in concert in generative ways; providing lessons, ideas, and possibilities benefiting of all. In this chapter we will explore the local/global rift and follow with an examination of how one might translate missional effectiveness globally into effectiveness locally.

COMPETITION IN GOD'S REIGN

It seems strange in the church to have a sense of competition between Christian organizations working to build the reign of God "on earth as it is in heaven" (Matthew 6:10); whether this be one church competing with another, one Christian nonprofit competing with another nonprofit, or local mission advocates competing with global mission advocates. I (Gaston) always pause when someone asks of the Christian nonprofit for which I work, "Who is your competition?" The question is understandable, and the hesitancy is not in using business terminology to describe work that has theological and social goals. At one time I thought the only competition a Christian church or nonprofit has are other organizations who are causing harm instead of doing good. As time goes on, however, I believe even that is a false assumption. Those unintentionally causing harm while meaning to do good simply have even greater capacity for improvement. There are plenty of organizations and individuals in this world that are actively seeking to rob life from people as a means toward their own ends. How shortsighted is it, then, to see other workers in God's reign as competition instead of allies? To do so is to place ourselves in a kind of spiritual poverty, where we segment ourselves from others God has called to work for God's purposes. There is room for many ways of working together. "The harvest is plentiful, but the laborers are few; therefore ask the Lord of the harvest to send out laborers into his harvest" (Luke 10:2). Not all efforts are as effective as they could be, and some likely create more difficulties than they address, but the possibility exists to do more and to do it better. If the laborers are in short supply, and they are, let us not tear one another down but rather build one another up.

Of course, the above thinking only applies to competition in a pejorative sense. There is a healthy competition, where each pushes the other to be the best they both are able to become. The writer of Hebrews tapped into such a sense of positive competition in urging followers to "outdo each other . . . in doing good" (10:24 TLB). In so doing, it is not that anyone wishes for the "competition" to do less well; each one simply wants to be the best. In such a way, we push one another to greater effectiveness. This may seem like an overly nuanced distinction around competition, but the difference can be enormous. Organizations seeing others as negative competitors are usually unable or unwilling to learn from others, much less partner with them. Those seeing others as positive competition can freely enter into partnerships for the sake of a more effective outcome and to have an open stance toward learning lessons, pushing them to greater effectiveness.

ZOE's own story of organizational change is an example of how an organization can increase its effectiveness and learn to engage ministry in more sustainable ways. ZOE began as a well-meaning relief organization, as discussed previously. In some areas ZOE helped (medical relief and educational scholarships for orphans), but in other ways ZOE's efforts likely caused dependencies (food distribution in situations of long-term poverty and giving out other goods). When ZOE supporters reflect on the early days of this mission, there is some cringing, but it was the best way the organization knew how to serve orphans at the time. When ZOE witnessed the results of the work of a group of Rwandan social workers who were transforming the lives of children in much more effective ways, ZOE was able to see a more effective way to serve children and change the organization to come behind this better way to serve. Regardless of the perspective from which you are reading this book—whether as a volunteer, a donor, an institutional partner, or even nonprofit staff—you have more influence over how such work is accomplished than you may realize. When enough of the stakeholders expect efforts to have tangible, measurable outcomes, then the work will improve. The oft-repeated idea, "Even if only one person is helped, then it is worth it," is a kind sentiment and holds some truth, especially if you are that one person. But it does not excuse Christians from understanding that God gives us resources to steward, and God cares that such resources are stewarded as effectively as possible. Jesus' well-known parable of the talents, found in Matthew 25, underlines this expectation from God in stark ways. God expects and encourages us to anticipate a high return on investment.

For example, if an organization touts how many meals it serves, that is measuring an activity, not an outcome, unless there is an emergency, such as a natural disaster or war. An outcome in situations of long-term poverty, which is the vast majority of contexts, would be how many people moved on to a place where they can feed themselves. Measuring activities instead of outcomes is a trap into which many Christian nonprofits and churches fall. ZOE served tens of thousands of meals during its relief days, but the positive or negative impact from those activities would be very difficult to measure. In fact, it was not until after ZOE began working with the most vulnerable children that we realized the previous feeding programs in African schools were not even reaching the most vulnerable of children; those who couldn't afford to attend schools for lack of uniforms, books, and the small fees required for attendance.

WHO IS MY NEIGHBOR? RELATIONSHIPS AND BOUNDARIES

One mission pastor explained, "When God looks at the globe, there are no lines." It is simply a way of saying the geographic barriers we erect to define where the limits of the Christian missional imperative end are not God's boundaries but ours. When speaking in churches about ZOE, this is a common hurdle. Someone in the group inevitably gives voice to a concern shared by many others in the room: "We have poverty right here in our own city; why should we be ministering to orphans halfway across the globe if we have poverty right on our doorsteps?" The question is legitimate in that it reflects a real desire to fulfill God's call to missional outreach. It is asked by people who want to help but may feel overwhelmed by the needs surrounding them. If there are limited resources (and this is often a false assumption, in most Western contexts), should we not look to our own before we look toward others? Certainly, a church that does not reach out to its own community is not sharing a compelling witness. However, healthy churches take a both/and approach. They reach out to those in their own areas but also reach out globally. The reasoning is that Christians reach out to all God's children, to all people loved by God. Erecting barriers to define where responsibility ends proves to be a false exercise.

Jesus addressed this very question in the parable of the good Samaritan (Luke 10:25–37). An expert in the law, wanting to test Jesus, asked him this loaded question: "What must I do to inherit eternal life?" Jesus deftly had him answer his own question, which the lawyer did admirably, using the same summary of the law and prophets that Jesus himself used in other places. It boiled down to "Love God and love your neighbor." However, one of the tasks of an expert in the law is to understand not only what a law calls followers to do but also where the limits of that calling apply. So if one must love his neighbor, one must know how "neighbor" is defined. What are the limits? In my local faith community? In my neighborhood? What are the boundaries of such a command? Voicing this question to Jesus, the lawyer then was the recipient of a teaching parable that told of two religious leaders who ignore a person in great distress, while a despised foreigner, a Samaritan, assists the person in distress. Once again the lawyer was called upon to answer his own question of "Who is my neighbor?" He admitted it was the Samaritan who acted like a neighbor to the imperiled man. In using such a story, Jesus exploded the traditional boundaries of who constitutes a neighbor. The teaching reveals a law that must be followed in spirit and truth rather than in any narrowly legalistic way.

MOVING FROM GLOBAL TO LOCAL

It is common for people to reflect, after having seen extreme poverty on an international mission trip, on how they are then able to see poverty in their own context more easily. People who have grown up in or been exposed to poverty tend to be able to see it everywhere. But many who have not been exposed to such situations develop a fascinating and insidious defense mechanism whereby their minds shut out the poverty around them. Engaging with people in poverty anywhere in the world opens one's eyes to poverty everywhere.

One of the most frequently asked questions when presenting about ZOE to American audiences is, "Why can't we have something like this here?" The empowerment program sounds great to them, and yet, usually the questioners do not really expect an answer to their question. Their underlying assumption is that such an empowerment program would not work in the United States because of a variety of complexities, ranging from a culture of dependency to child labor laws. However, when I (Gaston) hear this question, I take it seriously, and believe the answer is "We can." Given the right group to implement the program—one that is willing to hold to the principles of empowerment—ZOE's approach to empowerment could absolutely work in the United States.

Why would one think ZOE's model would work in such radically different contexts? Because there already exist highly successful programs for adolescents operating in the United States with similar empowerment principles. You may think this is a joke, but it's not. The successful programs to which I am referring are gangs. By *gang* I mean a group of young people with close social connections, who band together for mutual benefit and power and engage in activities (often illegal) for economic gain. They feel themselves to be—and are, in fact—more formidable together than individually. The activities of gangs are sometimes brutal, and their effects often evil; but the structure itself bears some striking similarities to how ZOE is organized, almost like a photo negative, with ZOE led by the Spirit of God, restoring life, and gangs fueled by activities that destroy life. What is difficult to deny is that gangs are successful in the United States. In spite of every obstacle and effort to stop them, this social program continues to thrive, especially in areas of greatest poverty.

ZOE's empowerment program does not work because it is a wildly innovative idea that had never been tried before. Quite the contrary, every part of ZOE's empowerment model has been proven for decades before ZOE began. Some programs operating in the 1970s were more like ZOE than more contemporary programs. What makes ZOE's approach distinctive is how these interventions are combined in the context of a group of young people who assist one another for social, spiritual, psychological, and economic support. This need for community and the power of working together is not innovative; it exists at the core of who we are as human beings. Empowerment does not need to be innovative; it needs to be human, and working together out of mutual struggle is about as human as it gets. It is this focus on addressing what is most human that allows an empowerment program to adapt to radically different social contexts. In the end it is not our differences that are so stunning but the amazing similarities across social and cultural divides. We are created in the image of God, and that image is true across any barrier we attempt to erect.

When thinking of how to apply empowerment endeavors to one's local context, the challenge is more how to change the philosophical approach than how to design and implement the actual interventions. The context of a particular mission matters less than how to address the deep needs of people. Addressing the needs of people experiencing difficulties instead of focusing on the difficulties attached to people can make all the difference. To do otherwise is like a doctor addressing the symptoms of a disease without ever alleviating the disease itself. Yet this is precisely the effect of our attempts at applying relief ministries in the context of long-term poverty.

There are seemingly endless ways for a person to address the difficulties he or she faces, and every person has many interconnected challenges in life. If a ministry focuses on building up a person's resources to deal with problems, instead of simply focusing on one way to address one problem, then the possibility of real change begins to blossom. I am continually amazed when a group of well-meaning people decide that the problem poor people face is education, or water, or lack of jobs, or malnutrition, or, [fill in the next big poverty solution]. All of these are certainly problems people on the lower end of economic realities face in disproportionate ways, but to think these challenges exist in isolation from each other or that fixing one will necessarily transform a person's entire life is naïve. Yet many ministries attempt to focus on a single-issue, magic-bullet cure to poverty, instead of seeing poverty as a system of interlocking challenges forming a cage around human potential. If just one bar is removed from the cage, another simply takes its place. Are there success stories where people have broken free from poverty with assistance from a one-issue ministry? Absolutely there are, but these often have more to do with the drive and luck of the person than the one-issue solution offered.

Of course, the difficulty of ministries focusing on one-issue solutions could be significantly mitigated if ministries focusing on one issue were able to cooperate with other ministries addressing other challenges, to string together a system of comprehensive interventions. In practice, however, it is exceedingly rare to see separate ministries working together across boundaries. Even if such a situation were envisioned, addressing the various symptoms of poverty would still not necessarily build the resilience of the person experiencing poverty. Over the past couple of decades, numerous poverty studies have pointed to one important characteristic of poverty: it is not in its essence a lack of resources but a lack of hope that proves so debilitating. As posed earlier, if a person does not have hope that tomorrow can be better than today, then why work for a better tomorrow?

Three underlying pillars that make ZOE a successful mission in some of the economically poorest places on the planet would easily transfer into those living in poverty in the U.S. context:

1. trusting the people being served to make decisions for their own futures, especially with the support of a group;

2. understanding what the people themselves see as success or improvement;

3. involving local people, those who are served respect and trust, in the ministry.

All three of these elements speak more to the philosophy of a mission than to specific kinds of interventions. These core elements lend more to the success of the program than any other single piece.

TRUST THE PEOPLE BEING SERVED

One of the reasons ZOE is successful is that, again, the young participants make their own decisions. Such decisions are vetted through a group of their peers and decided upon after training and information are provided to them, to be sure, but the final decision belongs to the person being served. This is a powerful motivator to instill ownership by those benefiting from the process. People become owners of the mission instead of beneficiaries of the mission. It is impossible to overstate how important such ownership is to success. What makes the difference between someone walking through the door of a mission as a charity case or walking through that same door with dignity and choice is as important as any other single factor in achieving a successful outcome. ZOE's success is in large part due to the fact that it trains young people to make good decisions for their future.

What makes the difference between someone feeling like a charity case or having dignity and choice need not be complicated. Take, for example, a church serving a small community and operating a food pantry, giving food to those unable to afford nutritious meals. At first the whole process of disseminating the food is a little demoralizing. People come and are vetted against a list generated by social services. Once approved, they each are handed a box of preselected food that they can take home. Apron-clad do-gooders sort food in the back and then hand it over. Who is there to help and who is there to receive is crystal clear. Some of the volunteers begin getting to know the people coming in for services and start to appreciate how much the recipients deal with in their lives and how demoralizing it feels to be only a charity case. The volunteers also reflect on how much time they spent trying to weed out the "scammers" looking to get as much as they can—and sometimes then selling the food—from those "truly in need," causing the overall atmosphere to become one of general mistrust instead of joyful mission.

The volunteers, in conversation with some of the participants, then decide to make a change. Instead of giving food away and prepacking the groceries, they set up the food delivery location more like a grocery store. Food is bought and paid for by shoppers, albeit in very small amounts. There are "coupons" for those who cannot afford the five- to twenty-five-cent price tags, which the volunteer staff give out as needed as they interact with the shoppers. Some of the checkout volunteers are also recipients.

Food groups are set on different tables, and there are limits to how much from each table a client can purchase. Much like a food club, it is a membership-only store, ensuring that those qualified have access to the food. As in any store the shoppers can choose which food they want and which they don't. All proceeds from the sales are put back into purchasing more food. This transforms the atmosphere for both the shoppers (no longer "recipients") and the volunteer staff. To the onlooker it becomes harder to tell who is who—who's a shopper and who's a volunteer. As you can imagine, there is much more joy in the experience for everyone.

Of course, such a progression toward empowerment is not without challenges. In this particular case the local food bank had a policy that you could not charge for food, however small the amount, and this was a major hurdle. The rule itself was sensible, but there was no way around it, even though this effort fulfilled the spirit of the injunction. And there were still some participants who wanted to "work" the system, but having people at the checkout who were themselves shoppers proved useful, because they tended to be at once more graceful and more informed when enforcing the rules. There were a few previous volunteers who had enjoyed the monitoring function, and some of these folks found the changes a difficult adjustment.

People entered the door not as charity cases looking for a handout but as customers. Volunteer staff went from policing to assisting in the eyes of the shoppers, and you could not immediately tell if volunteers might also be shoppers themselves. The "store" began offering cooking classes, tastings, and nutritional classes. Eventually, one could envision having a shoppers' council to meet occasionally, suggesting improvements and advice. Having volunteers who are also shoppers begins to blur the lines between the volunteers and those served. When we afford people dignity and choice, all kinds of possibilities emerge. Of course, in such a situation, the whole enterprise must be held more loosely. The clear rules from before no longer held in the same ways. It was a big adjustment, on all sides, but there was more joy for those participating in the ministry.

UNDERSTAND WHAT COUNTS AS SUCCESS

It should go without saying that it is a good idea to consult those being served when designing a service for them. A good deal of ink in a substantial number of books has been spilled making this point. It is also common sense, and yet there are still too many circumstances where the clients are not consulted about what is done for or given to them. Why is this? One reason is that those served are not respected for their decision-making ability. The thinking, almost always unarticulated, goes like this: *Well, if they were able to make good decisions, they would not need charity in the first place.* Such thoughts, which spring unconsciously to the minds of those of us broken by sin, belie a fundamental lack of respect for those being served. It assumes an us/them mentality. Often this us/them mentality exists on both sides of the ledger. Those being served see those offering the charity as "other" as well. Certainly not in every case, but often those who try to "work the system" see their behavior not as cheating goodhearted people who are trying to help them but rather as getting back a little from a system that has kept them down in unfair ways.

To do a decent job of delving into the intricacies of human motivation would take more time than we have here. But we can point out that we all come to the ministry with assumptions, and we also are often aware that most of these assumptions are incorrect in whole or in part. Forming actual relationships seems to be one of the only ways to break through erroneous assumptions, and one-sided charity does not lend itself to the establishment of relationships. I would never have designed ZOE's empowerment program. There are many reasons for this, but primary among them is that I would not have thought these orphans and other vulnerable children (ages zero to twenty) could make so many decisions or have the skills to implement them so effectively. I would have judged African and Indian orphans, incorrectly, as needing assistance rather than having skills and innovative thinking that simply needed to be unlocked. That incorrect assumption is all that was needed to keep my mind limited to the giving of relief instead of having the hope of empowerment.

I remember too many times feeling as though I knew what those receiving services thought, felt, or wanted, and was completely incorrect. I was once part of a church that stopped supporting a local homeless shelter because people were forced to sit through a sermon before they received services. I shared the righteous indignation at what I perceived to be using badly needed food and lodging as a bribe to hear the message of the gospel. I am a big proponent of the gospel but find coercion a poor evangelistic tool. Then, on a whim, I began asking people who had stayed at that shelter what they thought about the sermon. I asked Christians, agnostics, and outright atheists. To a person, people felt as if that was the best part. They loved the sermon and felt in no way coerced by it to get the services. They enjoyed being afforded the dignity of hearing about deep issues of spirituality and being spoken to as if what they thought mattered. They cared not at all for my paternalist protective instincts over their sensibilities. It was a more effective evangelistic tool than I assumed. Had I asked the clients before, instead of assuming I knew how they felt about this part of the mission, I would have been better informed from the beginning.

INVOLVE LOCAL PEOPLE

ZOE has all local staff working directly with the children in each country of service. The reason for this is simple. Local staff understand innumerable customs and nuances with which an outsider could become familiar over a number of years but may never completely understand. Another reason for hiring local staff with ZOE's model is because the young people in the empowerment program see the ZOE program facilitators as role models. They see the possibility of themselves reflected in the faces of those who are assisting them. U.S. missionaries serving in Malawi might well be beloved for their work by the people, but they are forever "other." This does not mean they cannot be effective, but there are unique challenges to such a situation. Within countries such as the United States, there are often strong neighborhood identities. Even here, someone from outside the neighborhood may be viewed as "other," with a different set of opportunities and experiences than those inside the neighborhood. In such cases engaging those inside the community in ministry with those inside the community can vary from beneficial to absolutely critical for success. This does not mean there is no role for outsiders. Quite the contrary, there may be critical functions for outsiders, but such work may be more supportive in nature.

To illustrate this point I am reminded of two people who informed my ministry. One was the director of a homeless day center in England, named Kevin. Kevin was a Methodist minister and academic. He was also successful in working with a homeless population with whom he shared little common background. Knowing that I wanted to serve in this area, and knowing that I knew almost nothing (and that is generous), Kevin took the time to help me understand that I was an outsider to those with whom I was working. I remember him saying once, "Even if you sold all your possessions, quit your job, and lived under a bridge, you would not be homeless. You would not have a home, but you would not be homeless. The reason is that you have education and opportunities. Any day you could find another job and lift yourself out of that situation. To be truly homeless is to have no choice and no hope of getting out." That advice has stayed with me for decades; acknowledging that I was an outsider in some important ways improved the way I engaged in ministry.

Many years after that, I was working in a homeless shelter in the United States and had the great privilege of working with a person I will call Mr. Parker. Many of the men in the shelter had colorful pasts that included incarceration, addiction, and other unsavory experiences, to which, as a young Methodist minister, I was unlikely ever to fully relate, unless my life took some very interesting turns. Mr. Parker did have relatable experiences with the residents, from back in what he called the days when he was a rock star. That was a euphemism for his addiction to crack cocaine and the difficulties stemming from that addiction. There were ways I could be of assistance to the men of the shelter, but Mr. Parker was able to minister to these men going through the dark night of their souls on a deeper level than I ever could. I had a role to play, but Mr. Parker could have conversations I could not. He carried an authority and trust I did not. Mr. Parker had an instant credibility with the residents that I never could.

There are many more things that bind us together as humanity than there are things that separate us. In God there is neither Jew nor Greek, slave nor free (Galatians 3:28), but there are those who are able to speak to experience not as sympathizers but as empathizers. Mr. Parker empathized, and not only was his ministry more effective for it, but my ministry at the shelter was more effective because I understood and appreciated the connection Mr. Parker had with the men of the shelter. On the flip side, when it came to raising funding from suburban churches, my credibility often exceeded Mr. Parker's in those contexts. We are stronger together. And to effectively live out Christian mission, actively seeking out diverse gifts for ministry often pays wonderful dividends.

CONCLUSION

How do we live out empowering missions locally as well as globally? There tends to be a "grass is always greener" philosophy when thinking through such things. Those seeing an international empowerment ministry say, "That is great, but it would never work here." But the converse would also be true if international mission people were looking at an effective empowerment embodiment locally. Empowerment ministries can take place anywhere, because the human beings being served are full of God-given potential. Successfully operating an empowerment ministry is about building people, not accomplishing a certain task. An important component of empowerment includes trusting those being served to make decisions. Having approval by a larger group often guides these decisions in a positive direction by taking time to see what those being served see as success. Rare is the case where a for-profit business produces a good or service without gauging what the market appetite is for that good or service. Do not produce something nobody wants—that is a pretty good marketing rule. Mission also must meet people's perceived needs. Here again, having a group-based ministry rather than an individual-based ministry may help ensure the perceived need is good. An alcoholic may have the perceived need of alcohol, so common sense must be applied, but generally, missions informed by what is seen as success by those served tend to have a better chance at achieving empowerment. It is also helpful to have those inside a community play important and visible roles in the program. The innumerable nuances and assumptions built into any missional activity are best understood by people steeped in such nuances. Outsiders can play a critical role in such ministry, but insiders have an advantage that can be exploited for building the reign of God.

In general, empowerment is harder than relief ministry. In most people's work it is easier to do something oneself, rather than train another person on how to do a project. However, people who consistently choose such a route end up working themselves to death and disempowering those around them. When we can build one another up, we are all stronger together. There are always needs on all sides of a situation. Those serving have just as many needs as those receiving services. When ministries begin to see themselves as places where people with needs give and receive from one another, and the helped become helpers, all receive from God, and empowerment begins to flourish in powerful ways for everyone.

QUESTIONS FOR REFLECTION

1. What are the most important things about participating in mission? What missions have been important to you? Your church?

2. How do Christians and churches compete with one another? When can that be a good thing? When can it be a bad thing?

3. In your experience, what are the goals for Christians to live as disciples?

4. Discuss the reality of engaging in ministry to the best of one's ability. What does it mean to be open to learning and changing? How does having a stance of being a learning mission or ministry affect one's perception of those being served? Of other missions or ministries? Of one's own ministry and service?

5. Make an argument both for and against the idea that "even if only one is helped, it is worth it." You can use the parable of the lost sheep (Luke 15) on one hand and the parable of the talents (Matthew 25:14–30; Luke 19:12–27) on the other. If you have a group, try dividing the group in two and each group coming up with an argument for the assigned side. Then discuss what a mature Christian approach may be.

6. What does it mean to measure outcomes instead of activities in your ministry or mission? Is it less spiritual to be results oriented? Can an extreme focus on outcomes or a complete lack of concern over them both result in less effective or faithful ministries?

7. Read Luke 10:25–37; what does this parable teach us about how our mission should be focused?

8. Describe the time you first witnessed, or experienced, poverty. How did that experience affect you?

9. Reflect on why someone might join a gang. What sense of community, protection, and loyalty do gang members expect from a

gang? What sense of community, protection, and loyalty do Christians expect from their church community?

10. If a successful individual lost everything, would he or she be in the same position as a person trapped in a cycle of generational poverty? How would it be the same and/or different?

11. What part has hope played in your own economic and/or spiritual development?

12. Good work tends to produce joy (not to be confused with simply feeling good or a thing being easy). What are the ministries you have participated in that have brought you the most joy, and what was it about them that made you joyful?

13. What assumptions and stereotypes exist in missional services? How do these assumptions shape the services? Are the assumptions true? If so, what makes them true? If false, why do they exist?

14. What difference could it make for the helped to become the helpers? How would ministry be different?

CPSIA information can be obtained
at www.ICGtesting.com
Printed in the USA
LVHW01s0021090118
562329LV00003B/4/P

9 780938 162582